AF575485

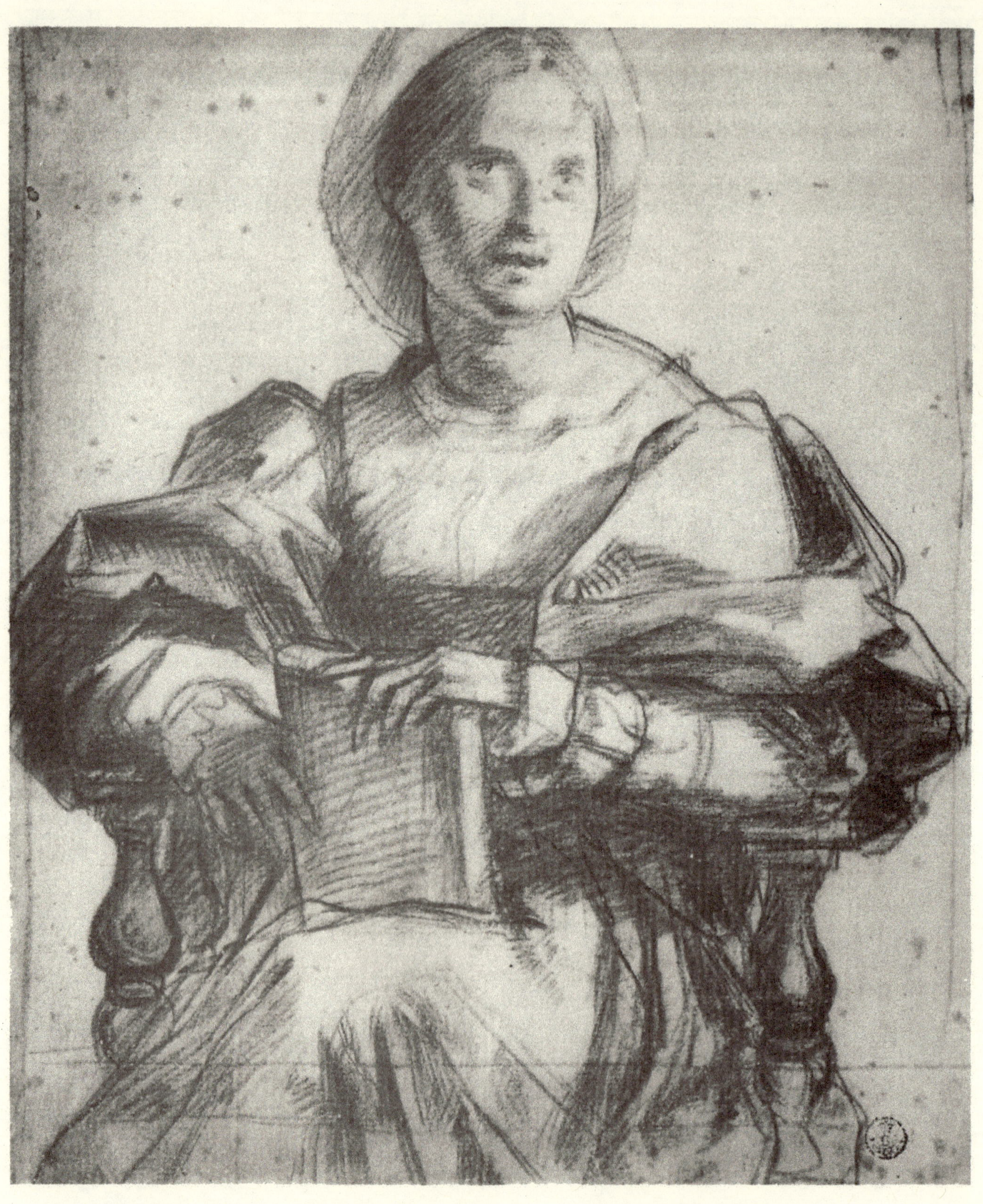

Andrea del Sarto (1486–1530). Portrait of the artist's wife, Lucrezia del Fede. Red crayon. 240 × 200 mm.

OLD MASTER PORTRAIT DRAWINGS

47 Works

Edited by James Spero

DOVER PUBLICATIONS
Garden City, New York

Publisher's Note

The works included in this anthology have been selected to demonstrate the variety of technique and attitude that can raise portraiture to one of the highest genres of representational art. On the most obvious level, a portrait is the likeness of one person created by himself or another. But a portrait also mirrors the culture in which it is created and can reflect the attitudes of the artist and subject toward each other and, more subtly, toward themselves. In delicately placed lines and touches of white heightening, Raphael portrays a young man (p. 14) whose individuality is made subservient to an ideal of beauty. Dürer, on the other hand, recording the features of his mother shortly before her death (p. 27), is able to capture the beauty of the human spirit in a meticulously rendered, brutally realistic depiction of corporal decay. Personality has no place in the portrait of the Duc de Noailles by Hyacinthe Rigaud (p. 41). Here the artist, most famous for his portrait of Louis XIV as an icon of royal power, is concerned solely with the status of the subject as expressed by his posture and dress.

Old Master Portrait Drawings: 47 Works is a new work, first published by Dover Publications in 1990.

Library of Congress Cataloging-in-Publication Data

Old master portrait drawings / edited by James Spero.
p. cm.—(Dover art library)
ISBN-13: 978-0-486-26364-9
ISBN-10: 0-486-26364-9
1. Portrait drawing. I. Spero, James. II. Series.
NC773.04 1990 90-3268
743.94—dc20 CIP

Printed in Canada
26364917 2025
www.doverpublications.com

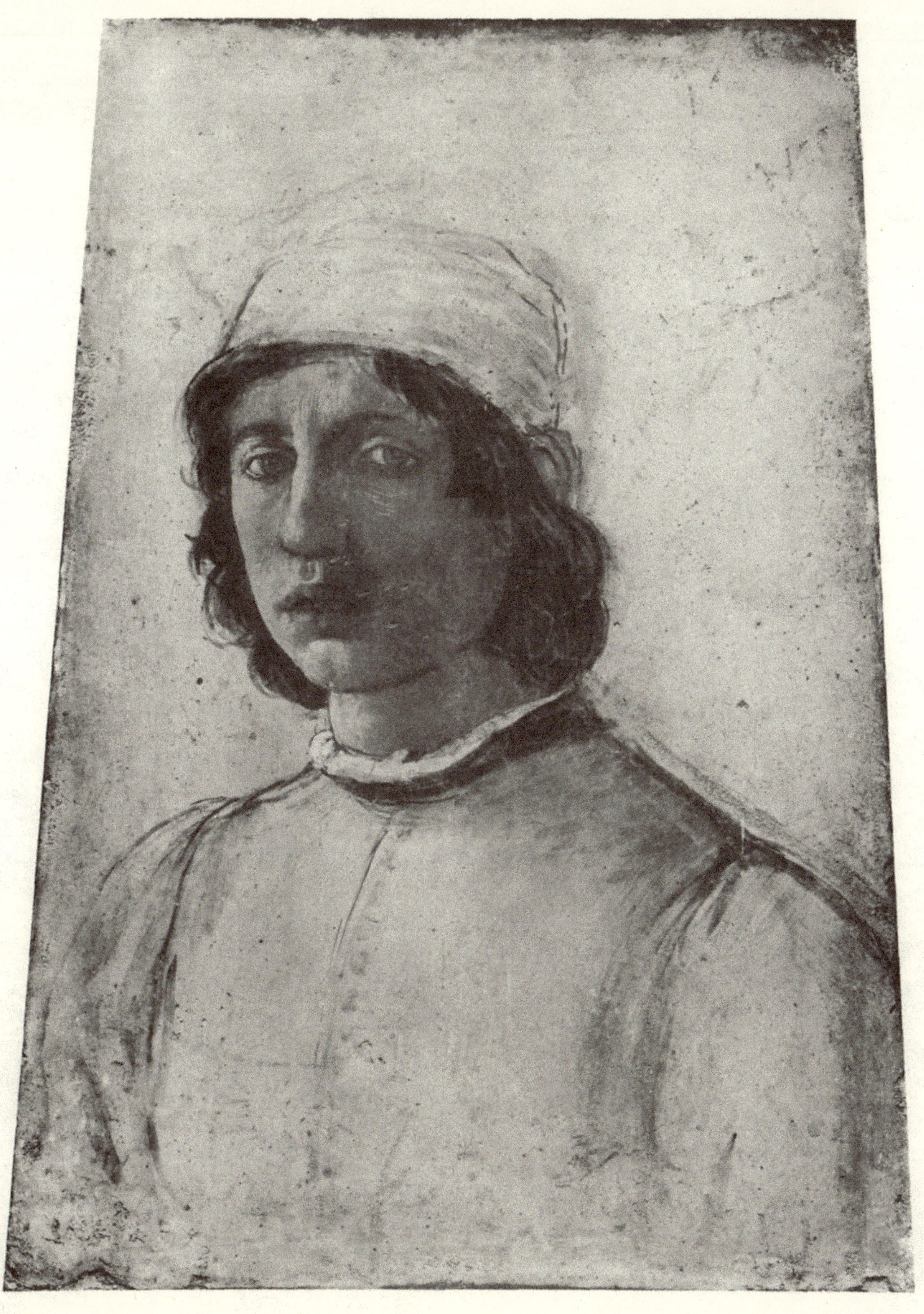

Filippino Lippi (ca. 1457–1504). Self-portrait (?). Tempera on roof tile.

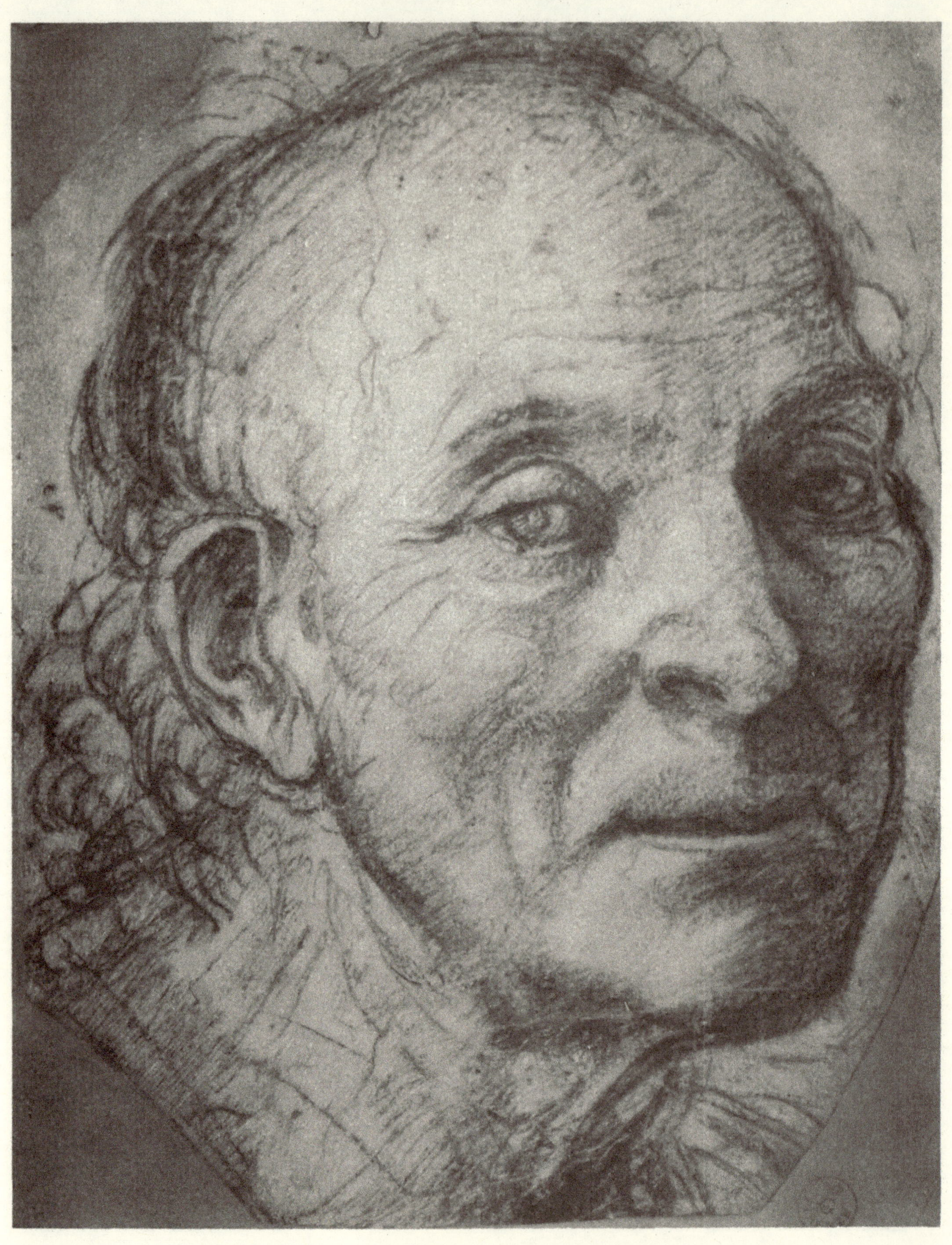

Luca Signorelli (1441/50–1523). Head of an old man. Black chalk. 250 × 170 mm.

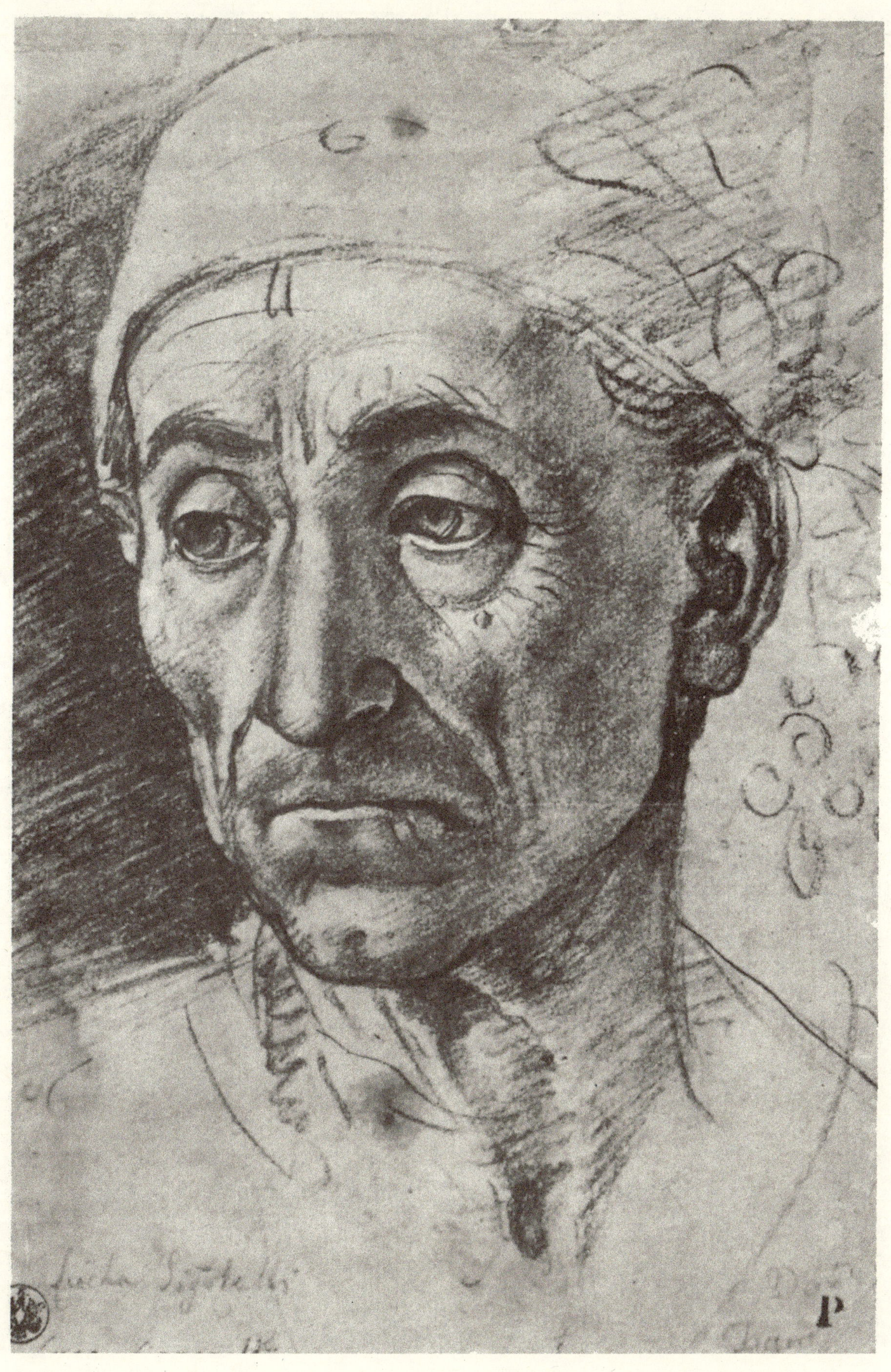

Luca Signorelli (1441/50–1504). Head of an old man. Black chalk. 236 × 156 mm.

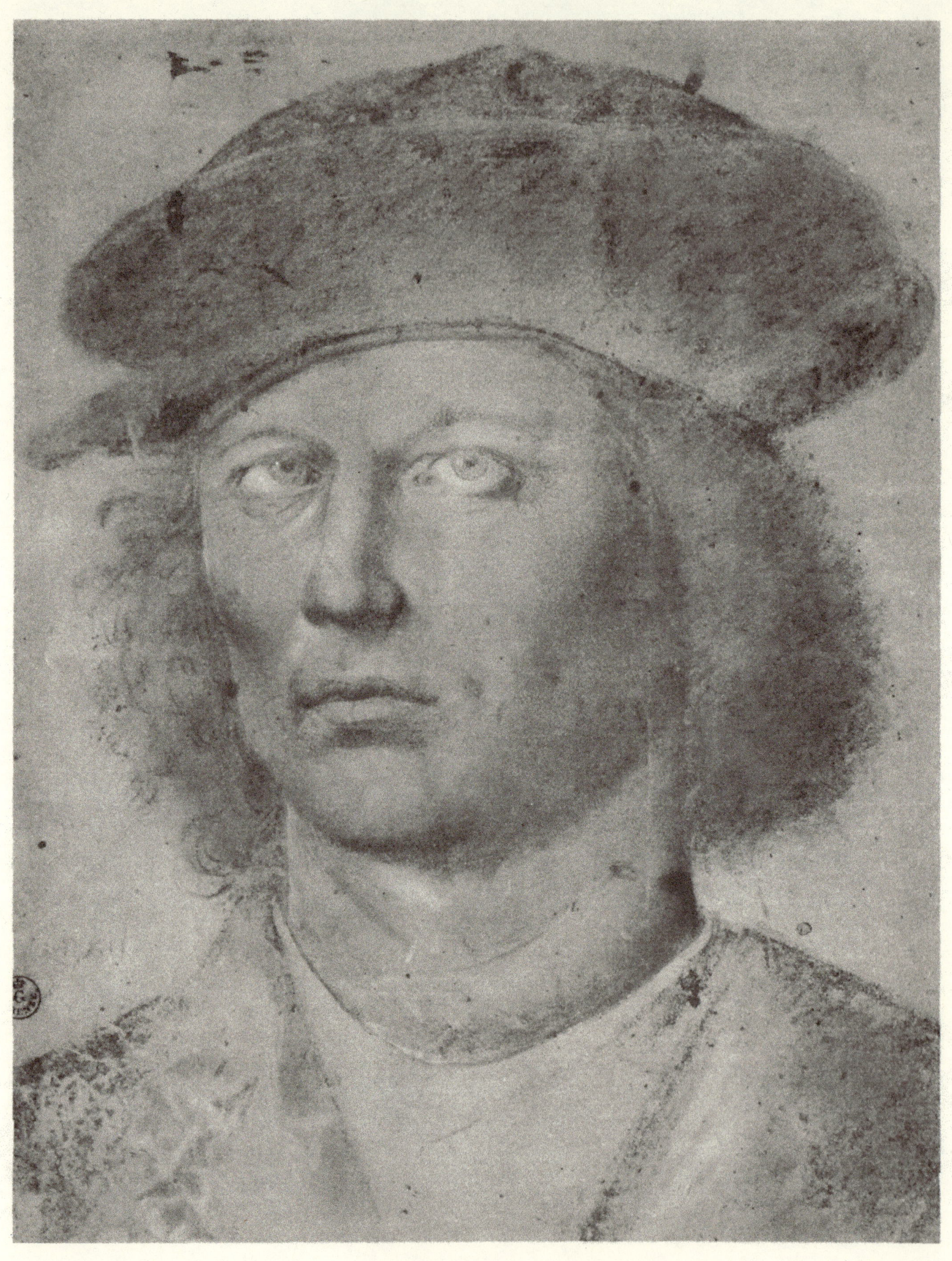

Boccaccio Boccaccino (ca. 1467–1524/25). Portrait of a man. Red and black chalk on colored paper with some white heightening. 285 × 162 mm.

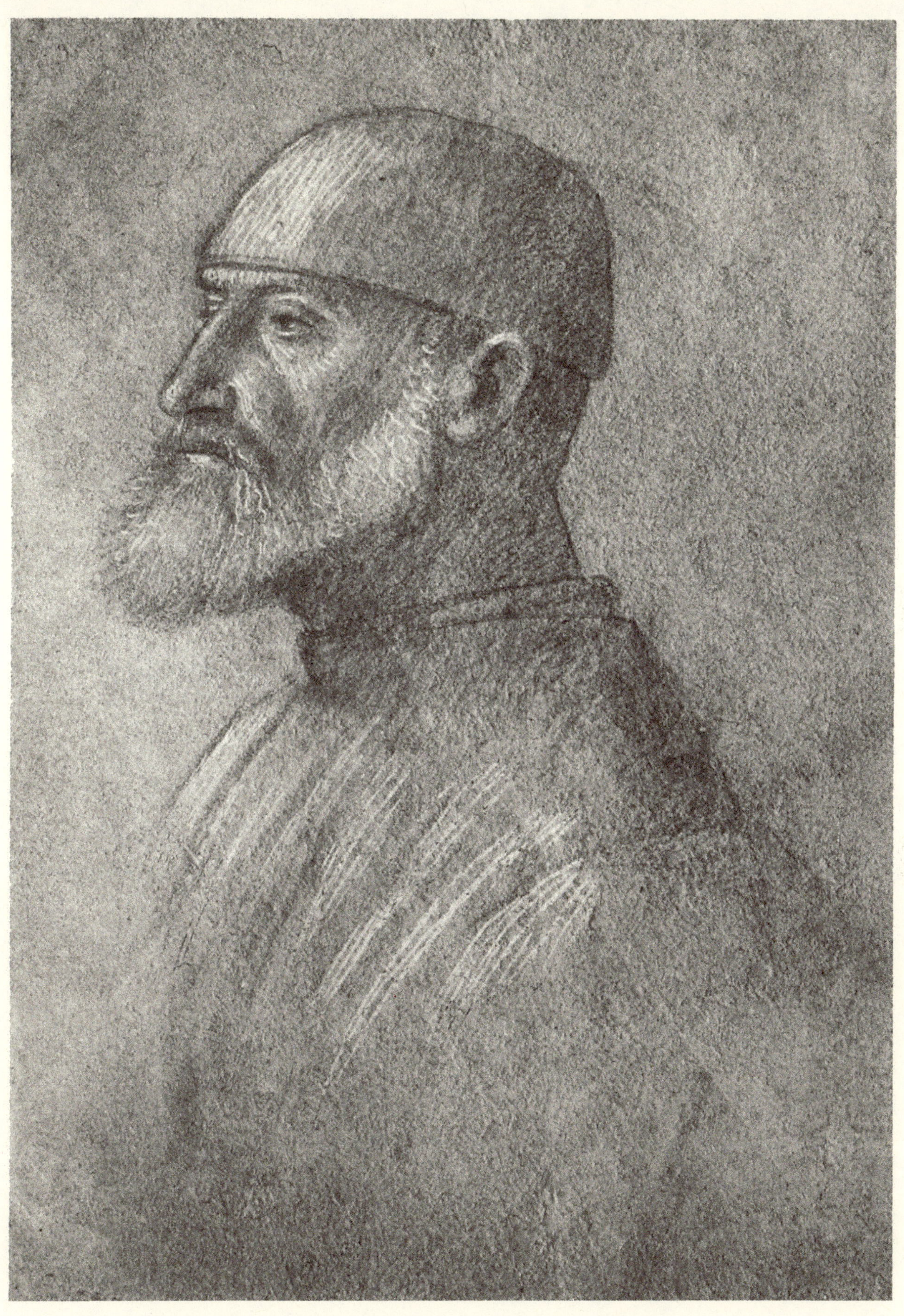

Vittore Carpaccio (ca. 1455–1526). Head of a bearded man. Brush and brown wash, some black chalk heightened with white, on blue paper. 265 × 186 mm.

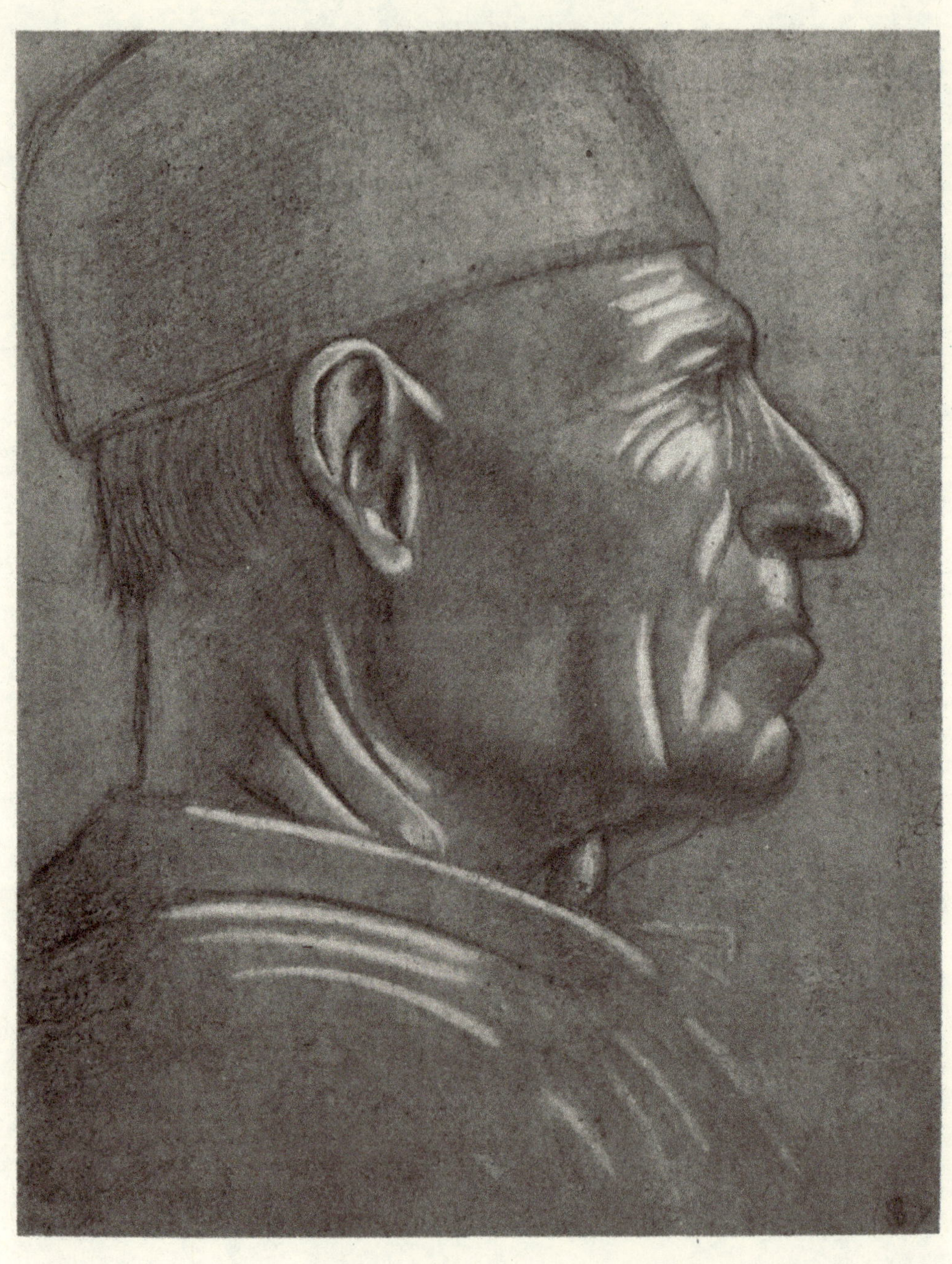

Ghirlandaio (Domenico di Tommaso Bigordi; 1449–1494). Portrait of an elderly man. Silverpoint, heightened with white, on pink paper. 170 × 130 mm.

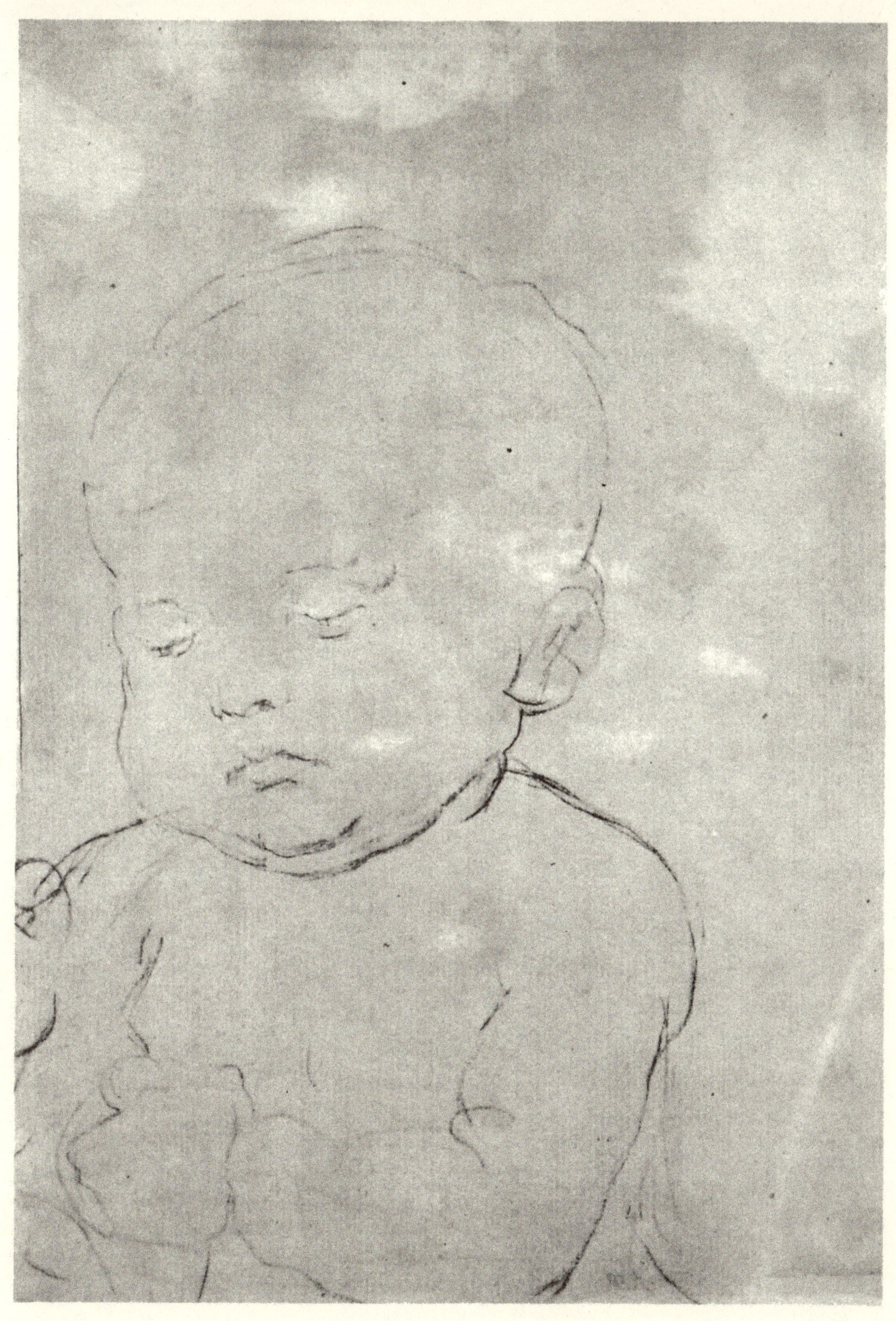

Andrea del Verrocchio (Andrea di Cione; 1435–1488). Bust of a child. Black chalk on white paper. 280 × 200 mm.

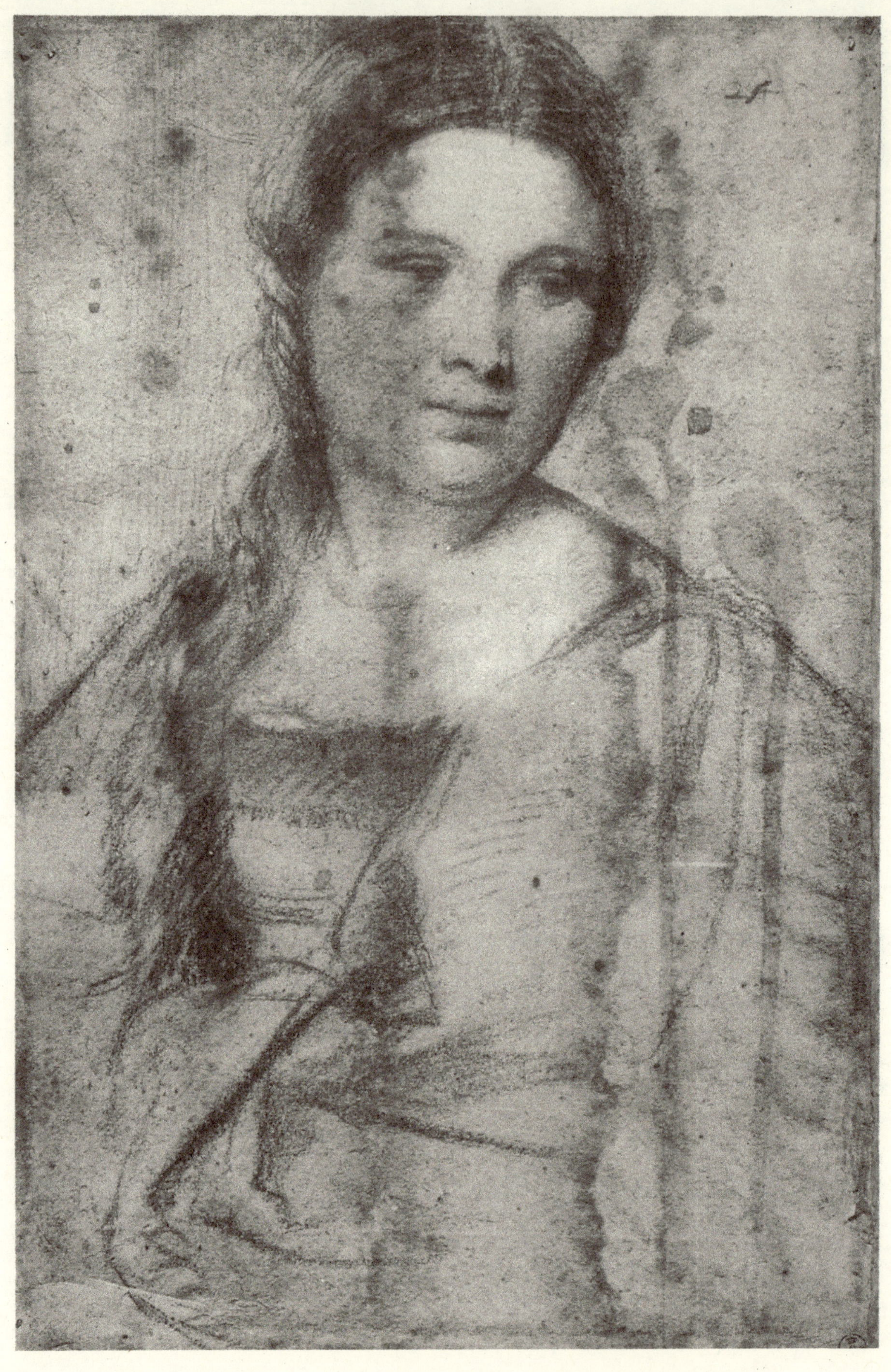

Titian (Tiziano Vecellio; ca. 1487–1576). Portrait of a woman. Black and white chalk on tinted paper. 415 × 270 mm.

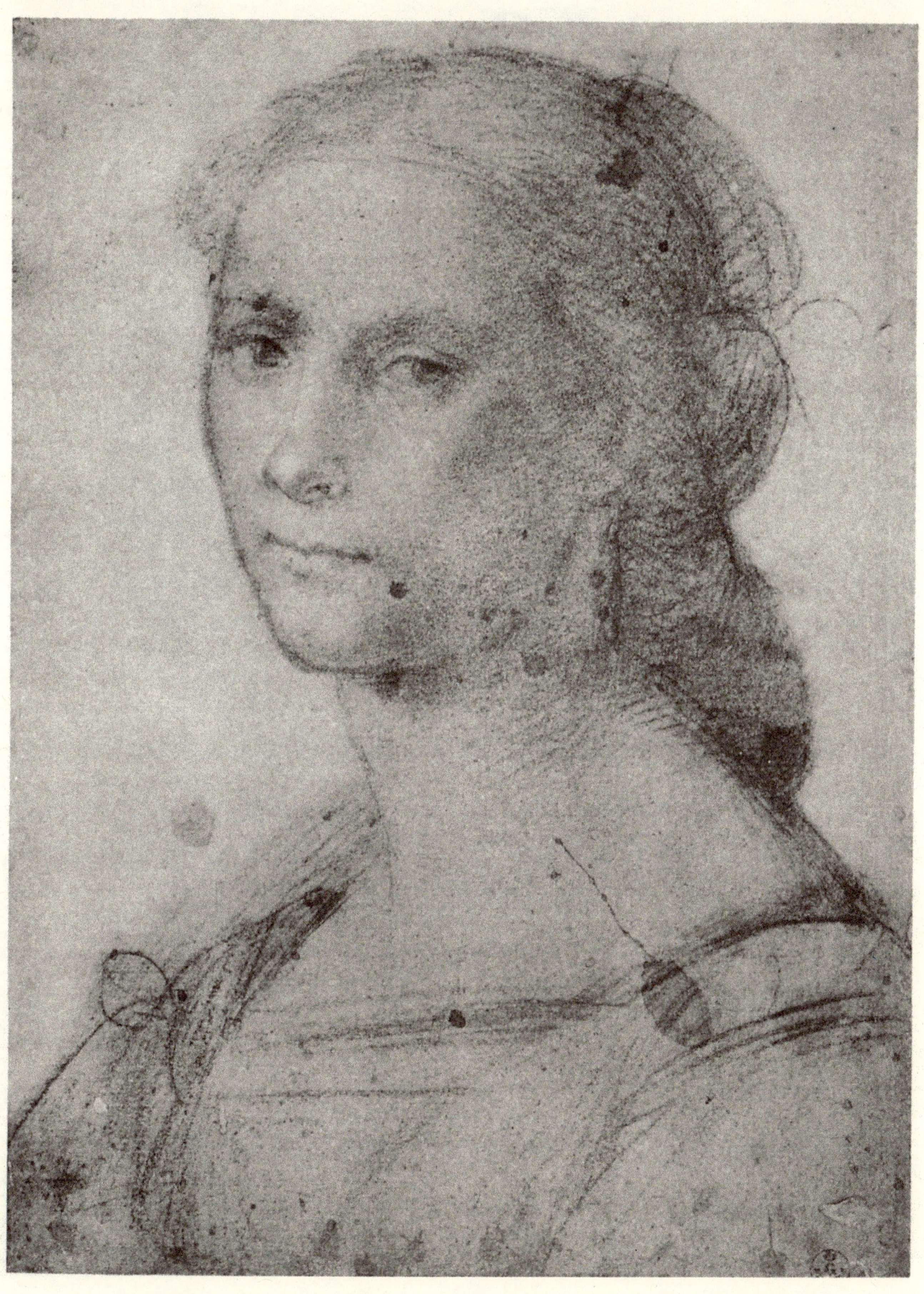

Fra Bartolommeo (Baccio Della Porta; ca. 1472–1517). Head of a woman. Black chalk.
399 × 290 mm.

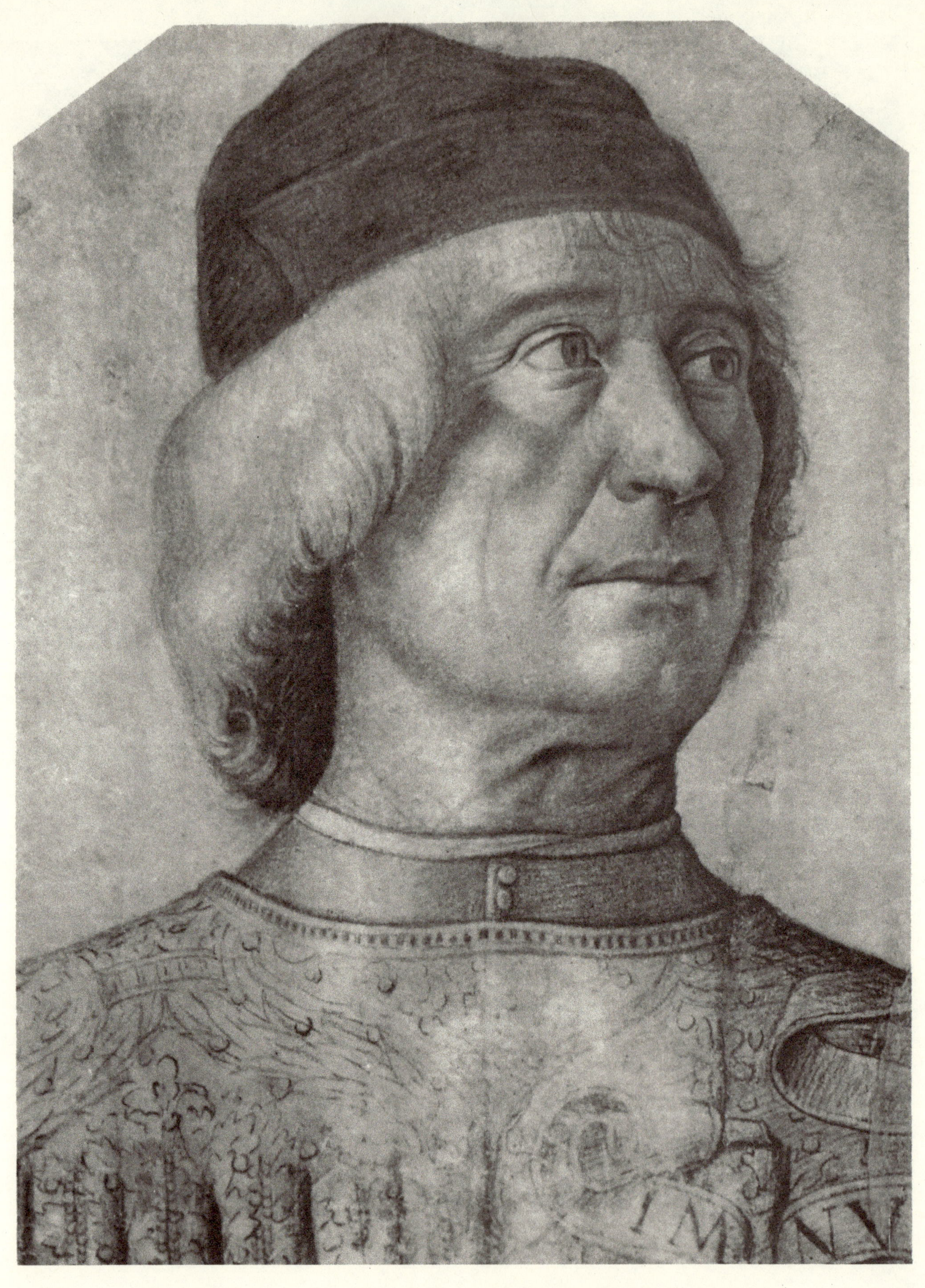

Andrea Mantegna (1431–1506). Head of a man. Black chalk with wash on paper. 392 × 280 mm.

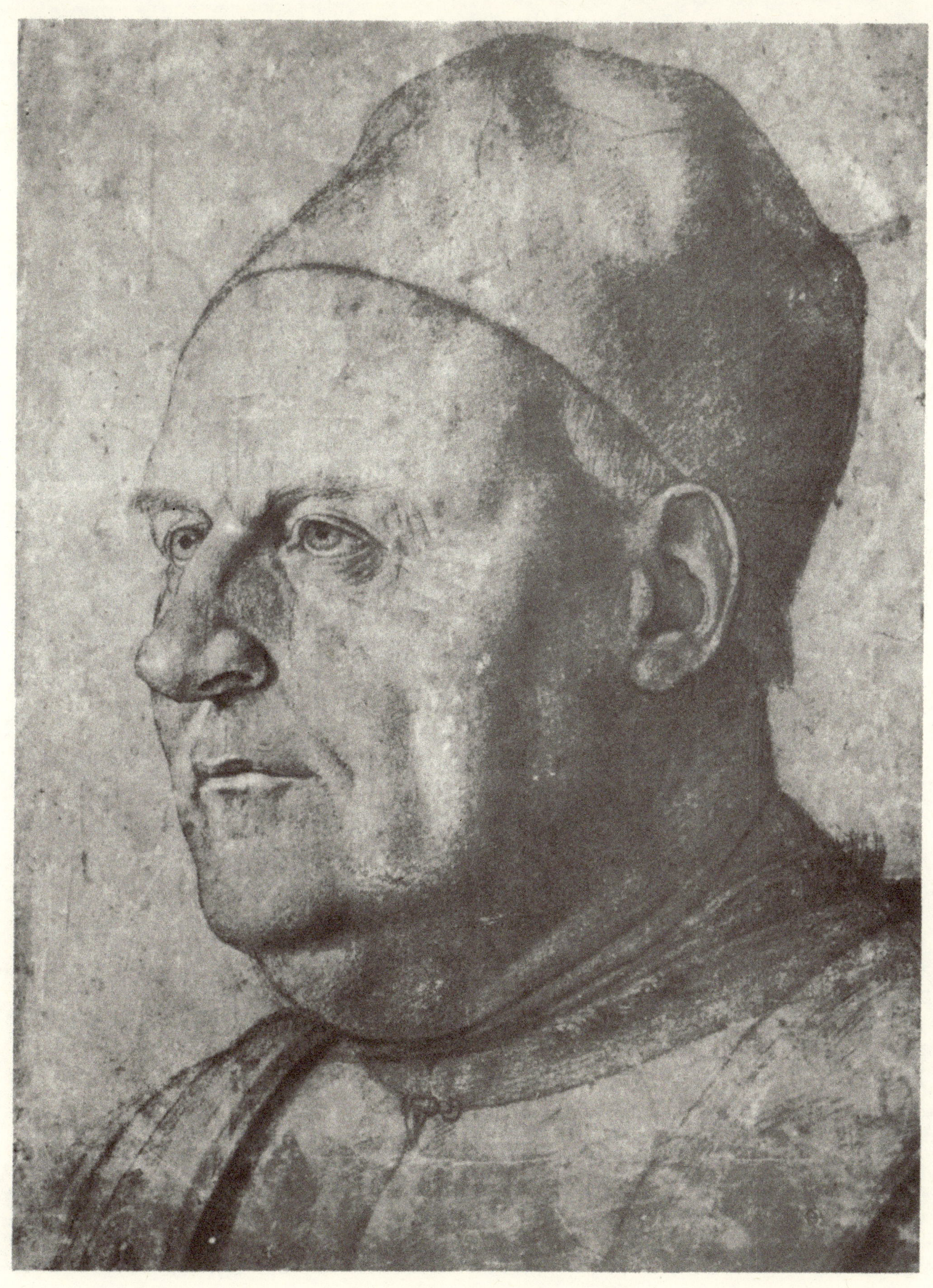

Francesco di Alberto Bonsignori (1455–1519). Head of a man. Black chalk retouched with charcoal on brown paper. 360 × 262 mm.

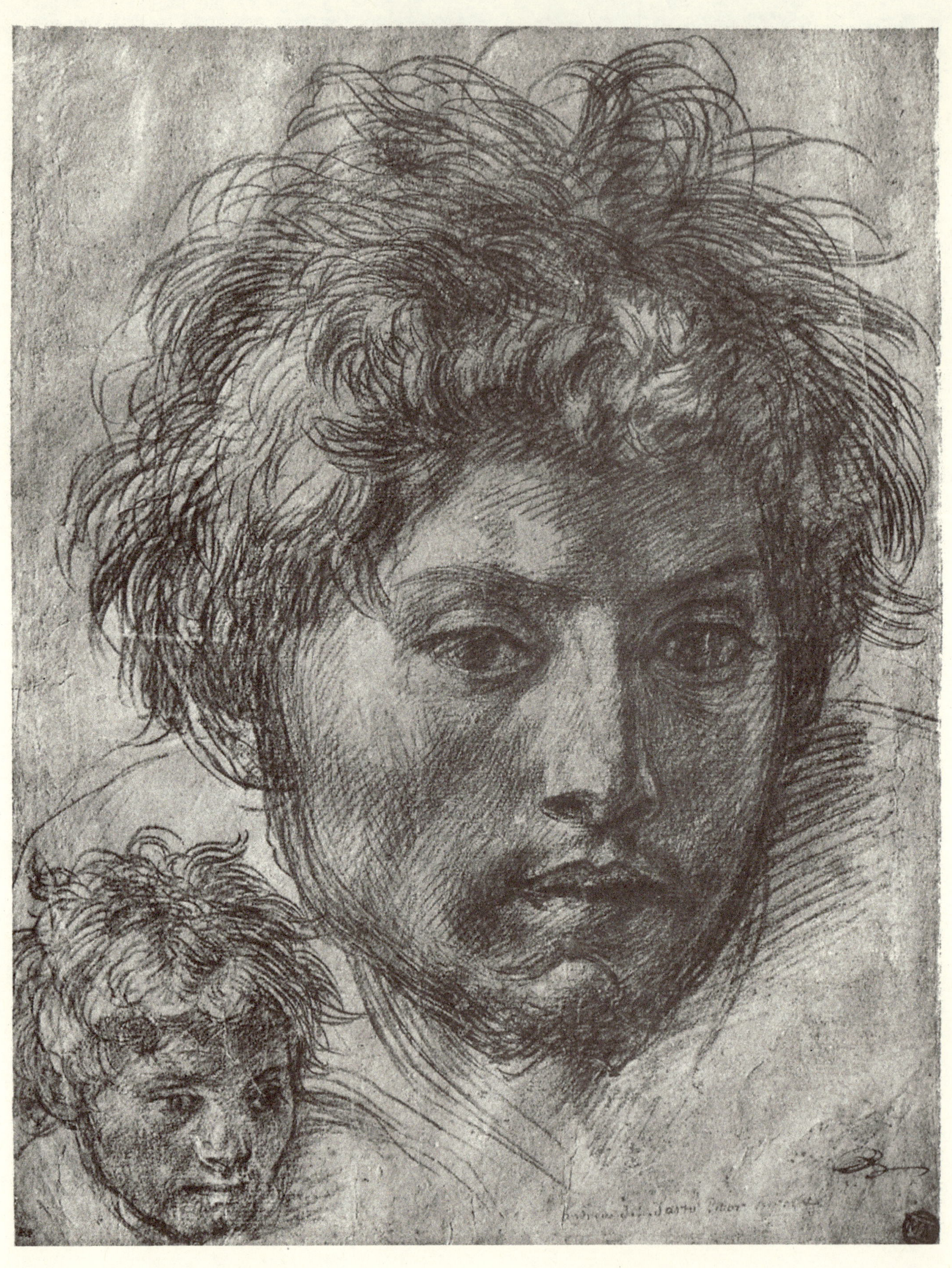

Andrea del Sarto (1486–1530). Head of a young man. Red chalk. 330 × 260 mm.

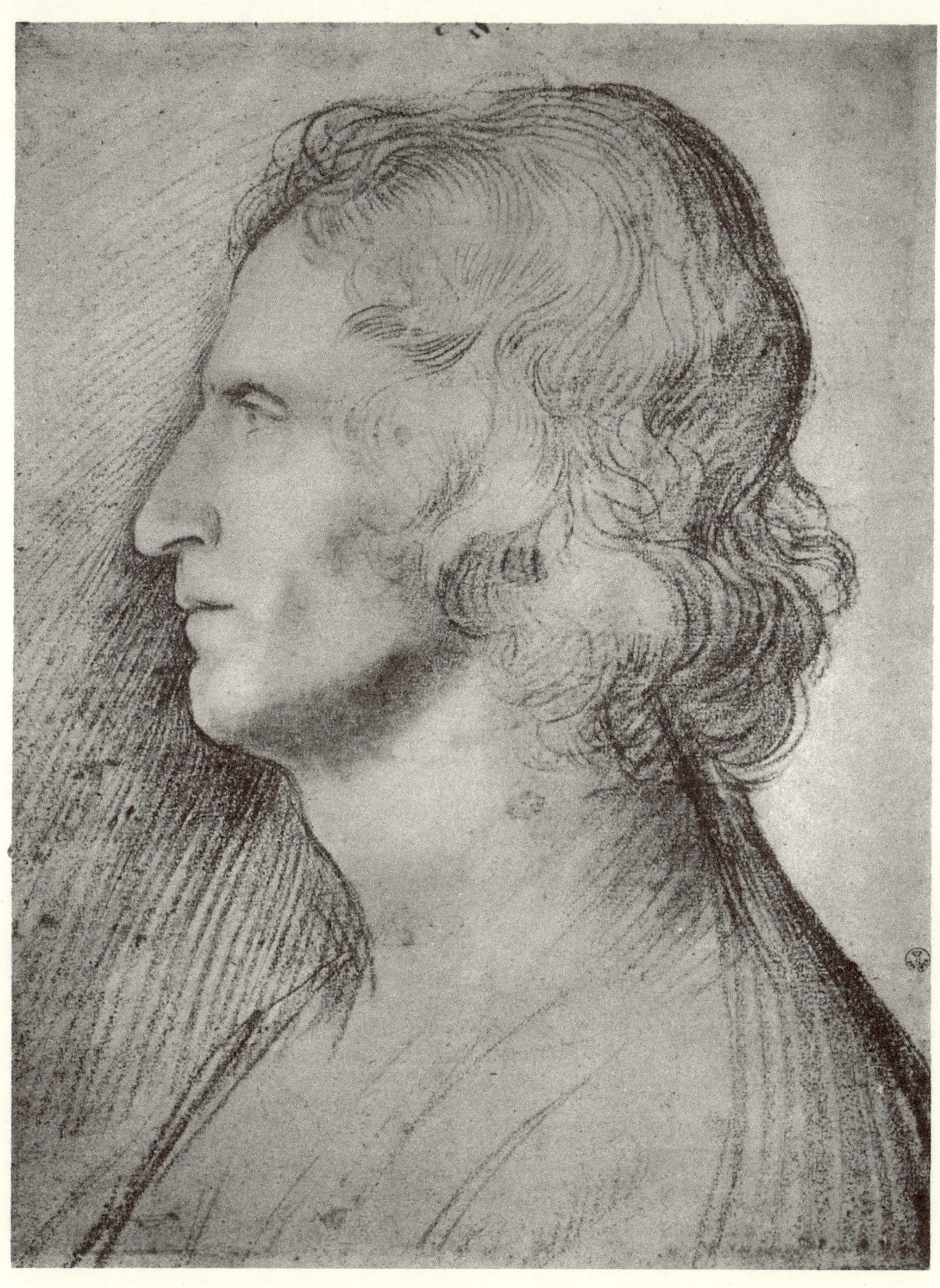

Pordenone (Giovanni Antonio Regillo; 1483–1536). Portrait of a man in profile. Black chalk on cerulean paper. 430 × 320 mm.

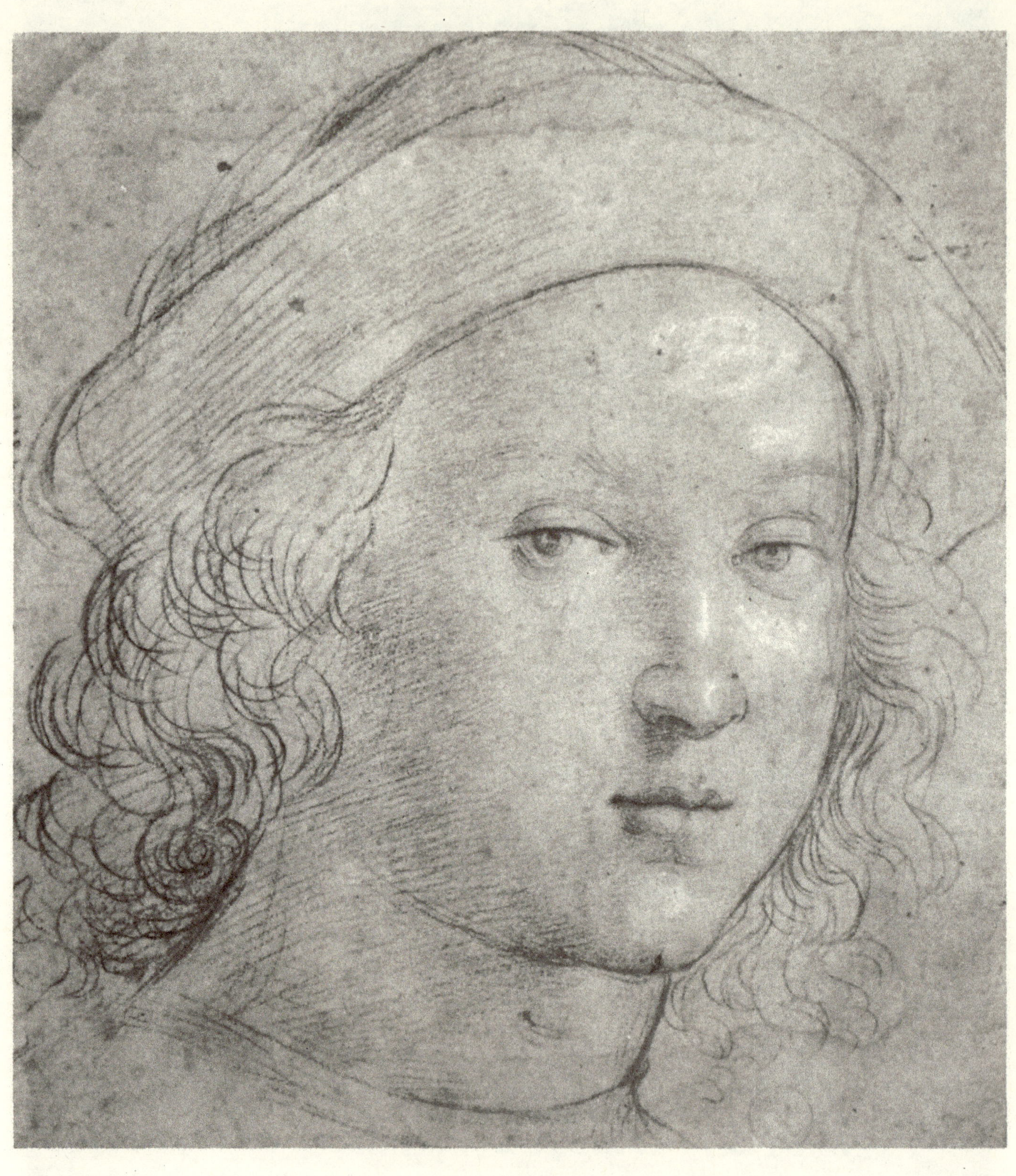

Raphael (Raffaello Sanzio; 1483–1520). Head of a youth. Black chalk, heightened with white, on bister-tinted paper. 211 × 187 mm.

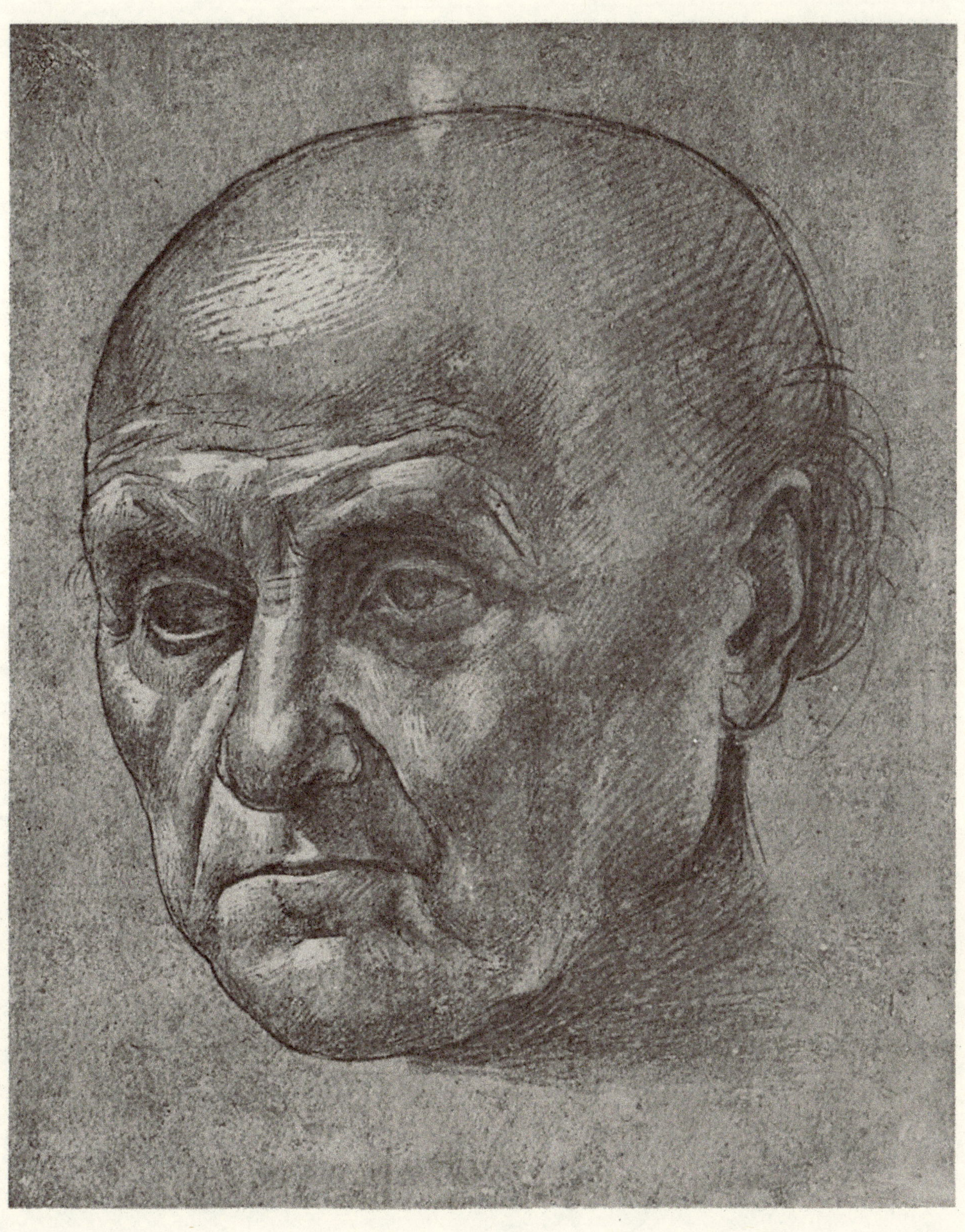

Piero di Cosimo (Piero di Lorenzo; 1462–1521). Head of an old man. Black chalk, heightened with white, on tinted ground. 205 × 165 mm.

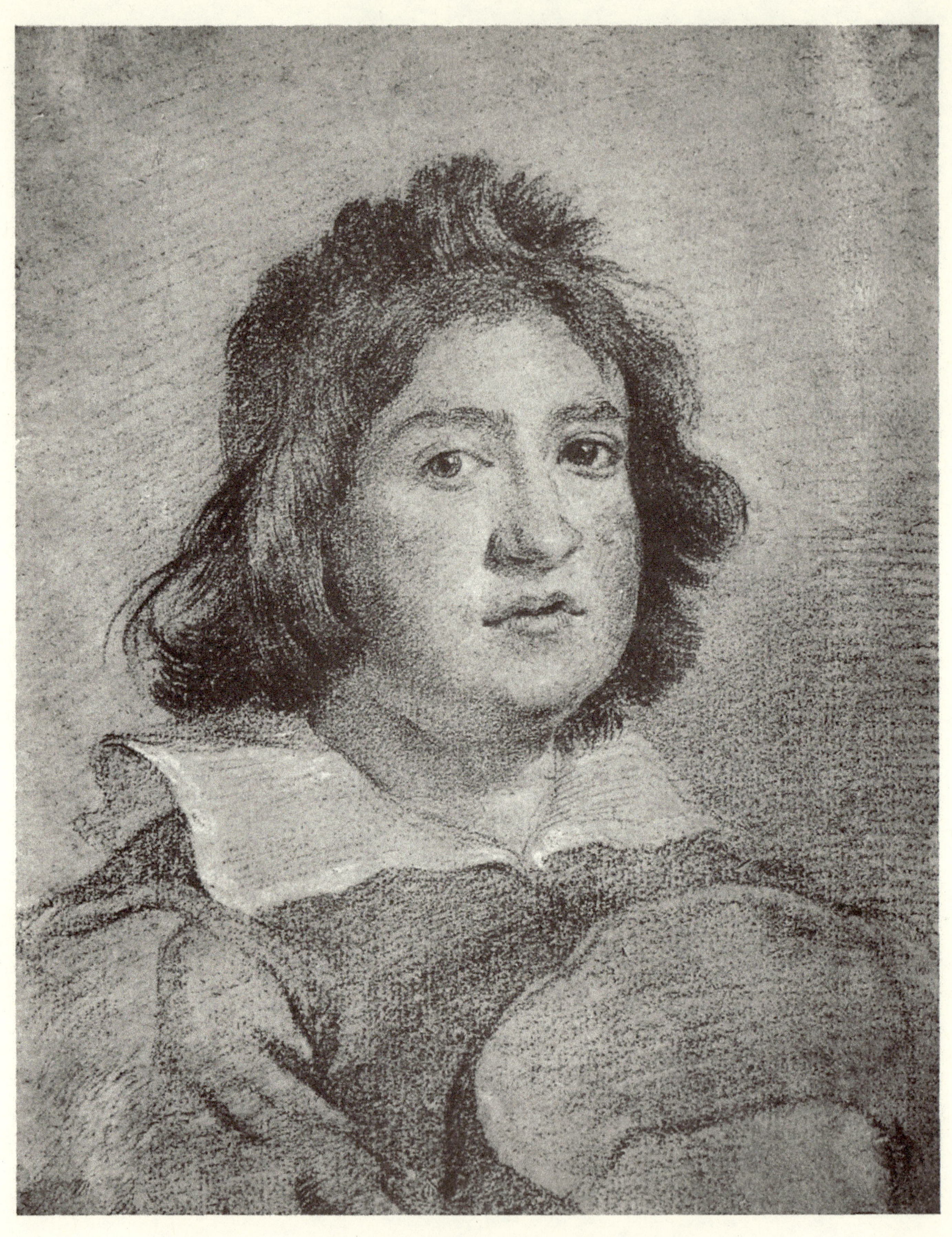

Gianlorenzo Bernini (1598–1680). Portrait of Pola. Black and white chalk, heightened with white, on toned paper.

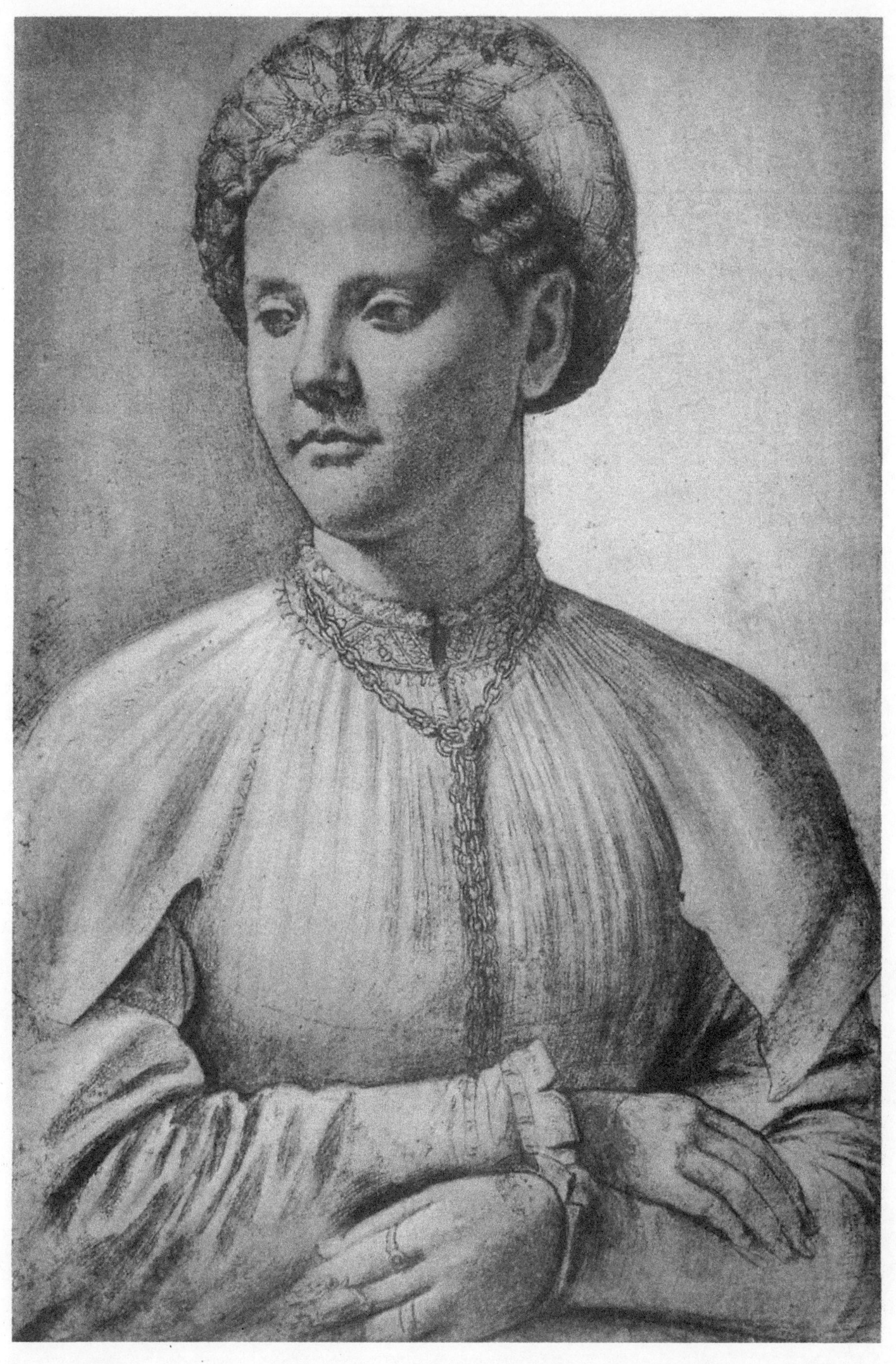

Pontormo (Jacopo Carrucci; 1494–1556/57). Portrait of a woman. Red chalk. 390 × 265 mm.

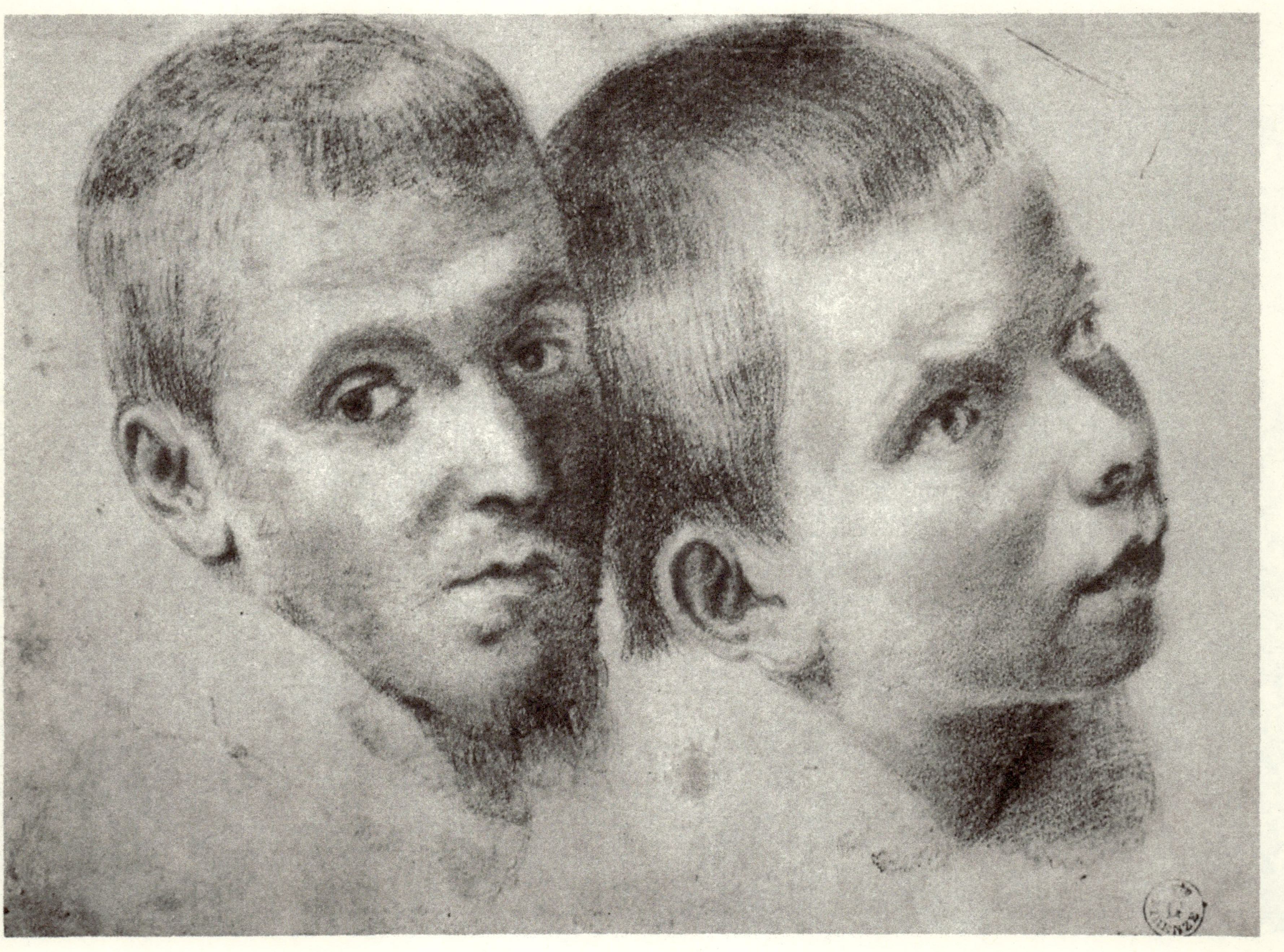

Cristofano Allori (1577–1621). Two heads. Black and red chalk. 255 × 195 mm.

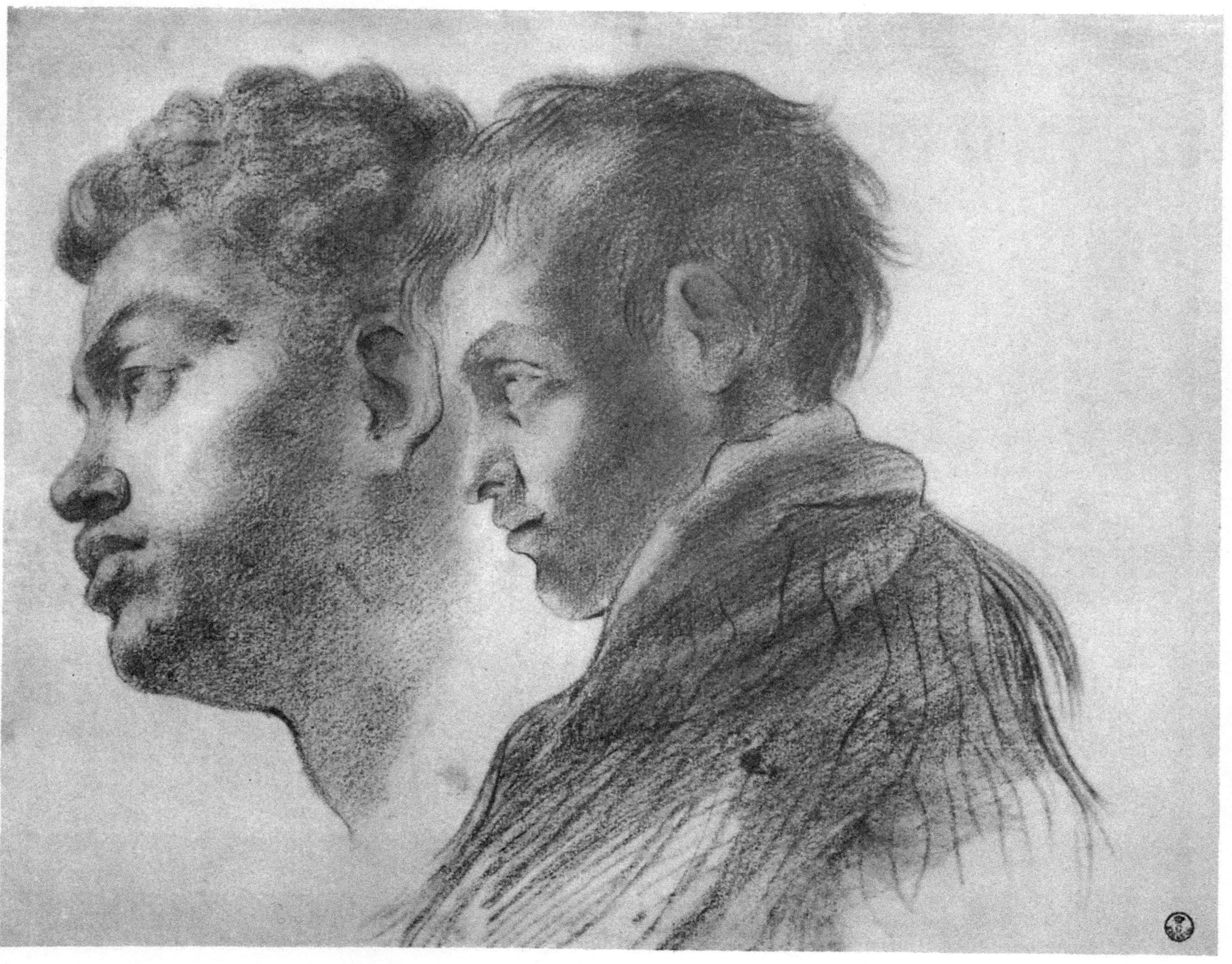

Annibale Carracci (1560–1609). Heads of a young man and a boy. Red chalk. 284 × 366 mm.

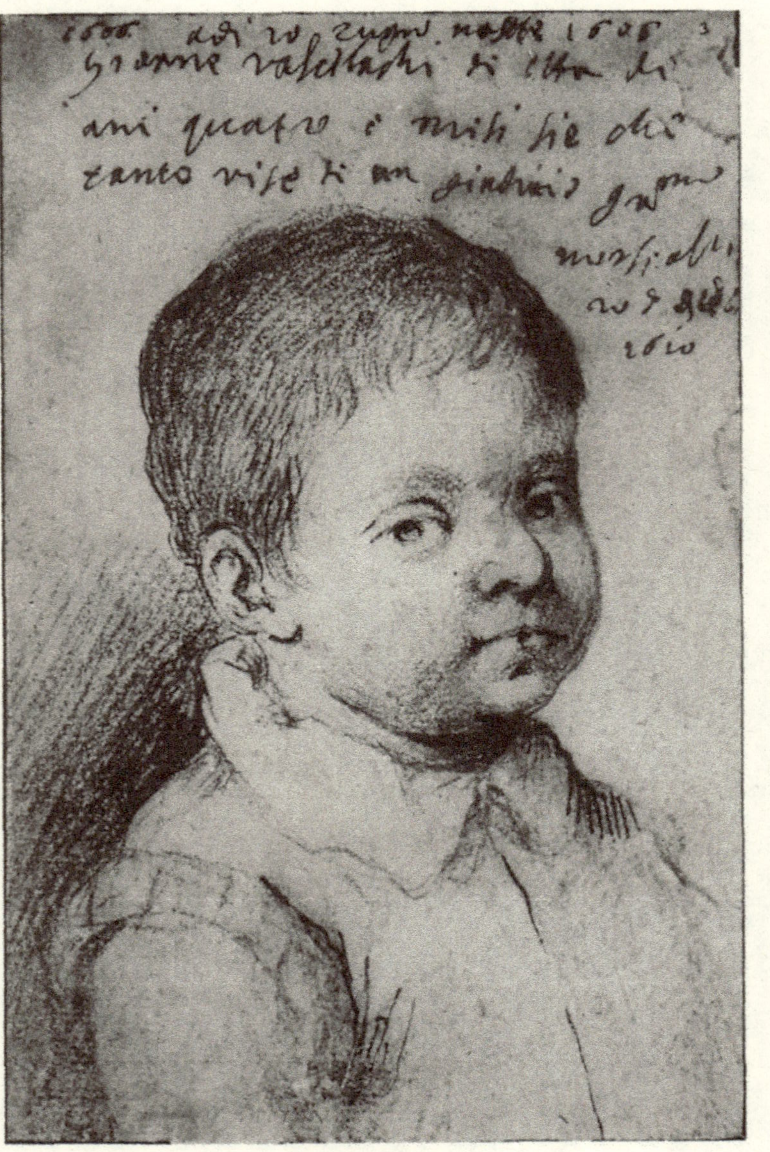

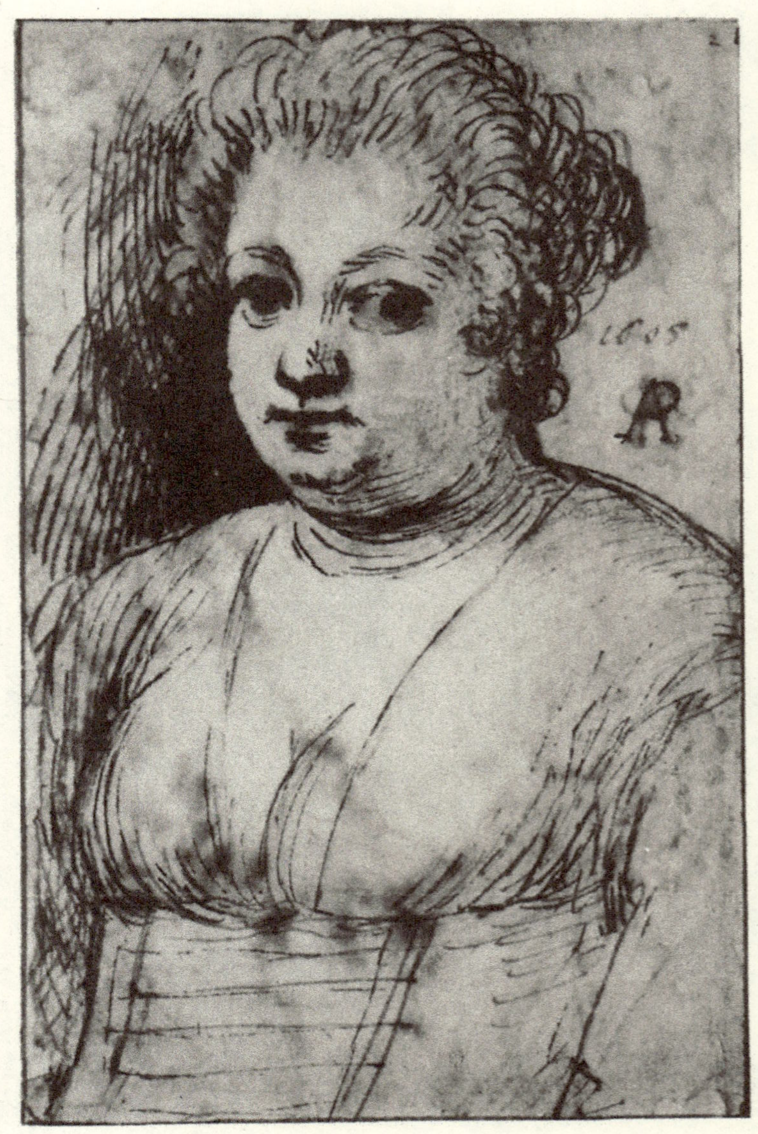

Palma Giovane (Jacopo Palma; 1544–1628). Portraits of the artist's wife and son. Red chalk, pen and bister.

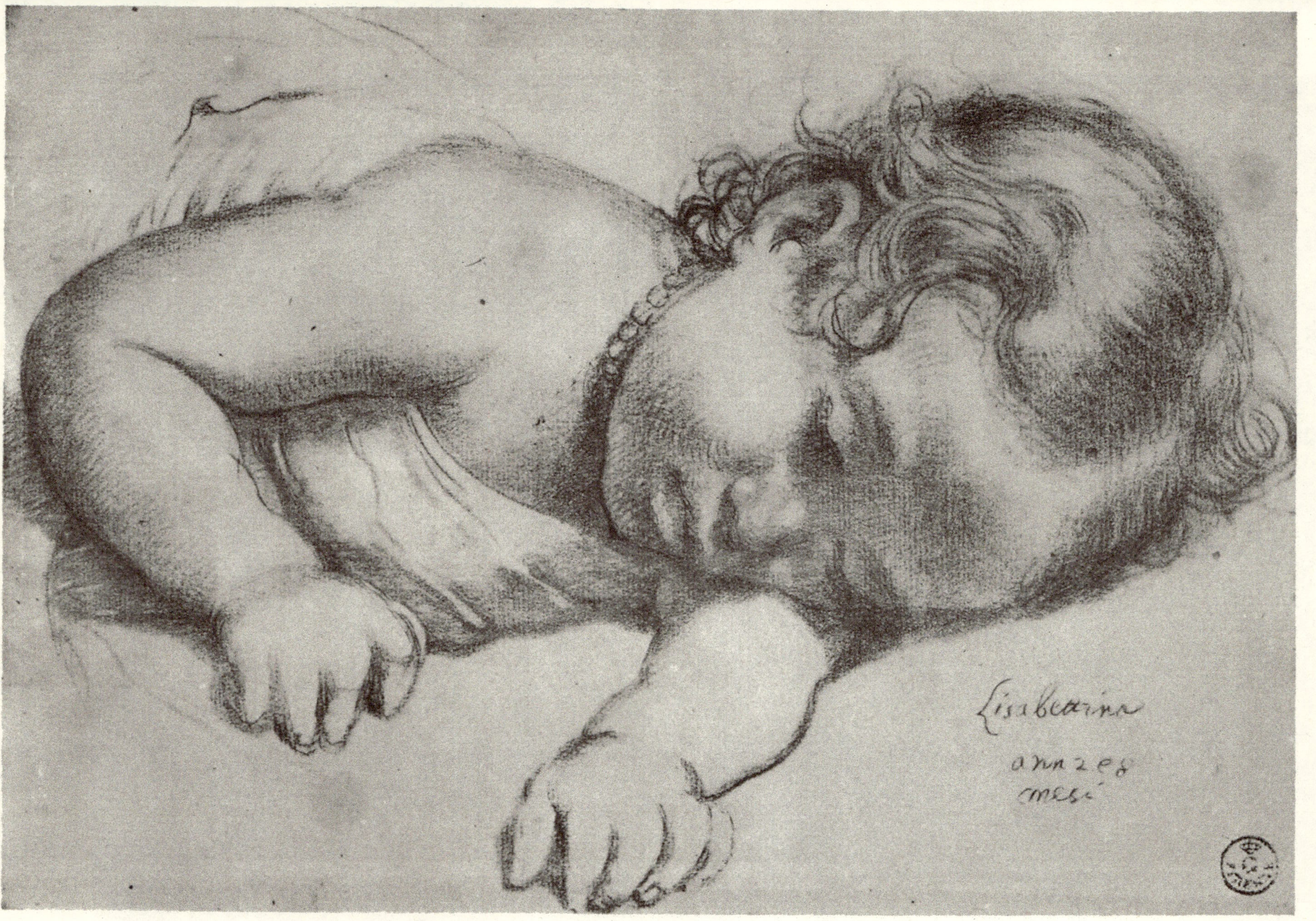

Matteo Roselli (1578–1650). Lisabettina, 2 years, 8 months. Red chalk. 180 × 260 mm.

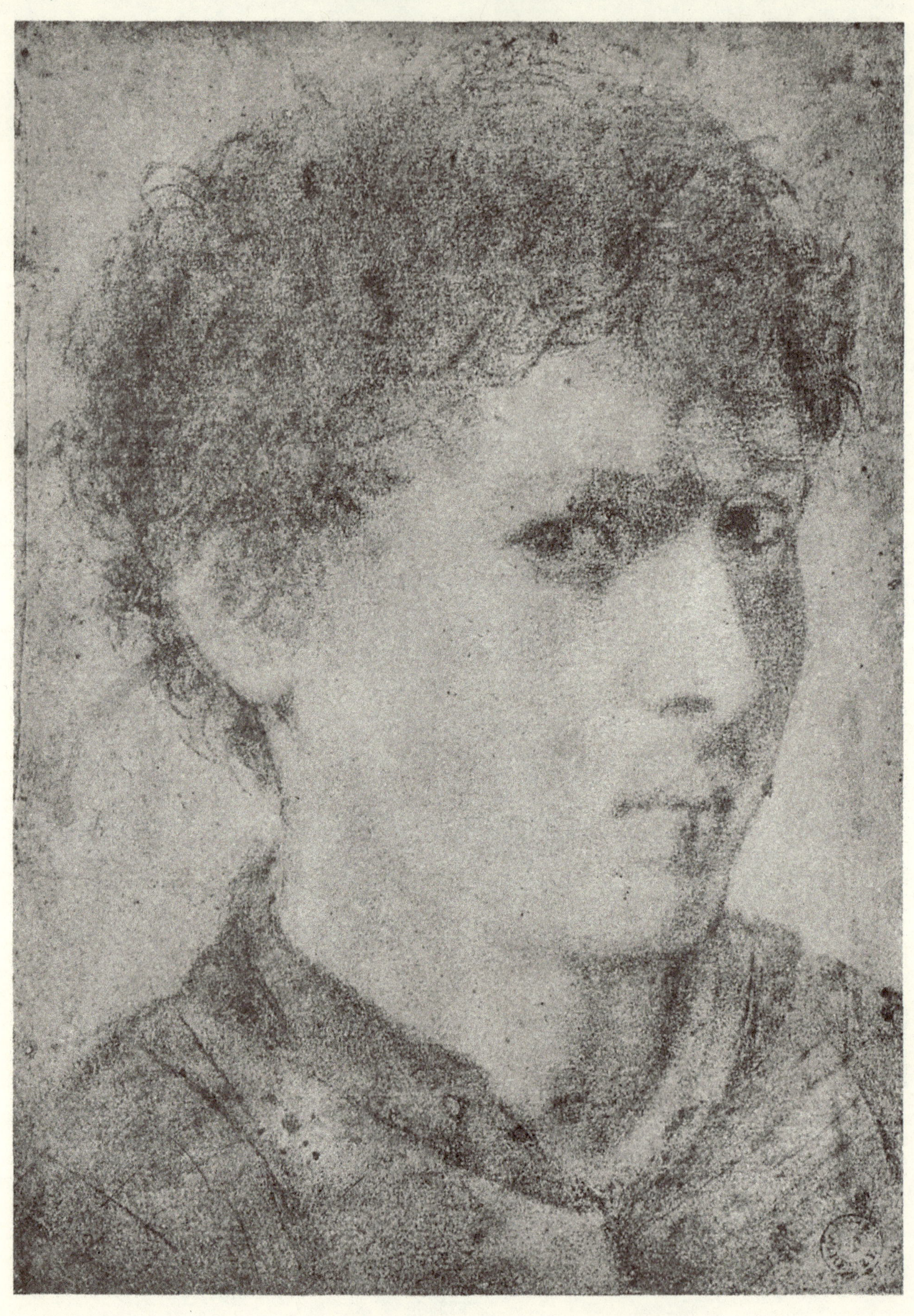

Giovanni Girolamo Savoldo (ca. 1480–ca. 1548). Head of a youth. Black crayon on tinted paper. 255 × 180 mm.

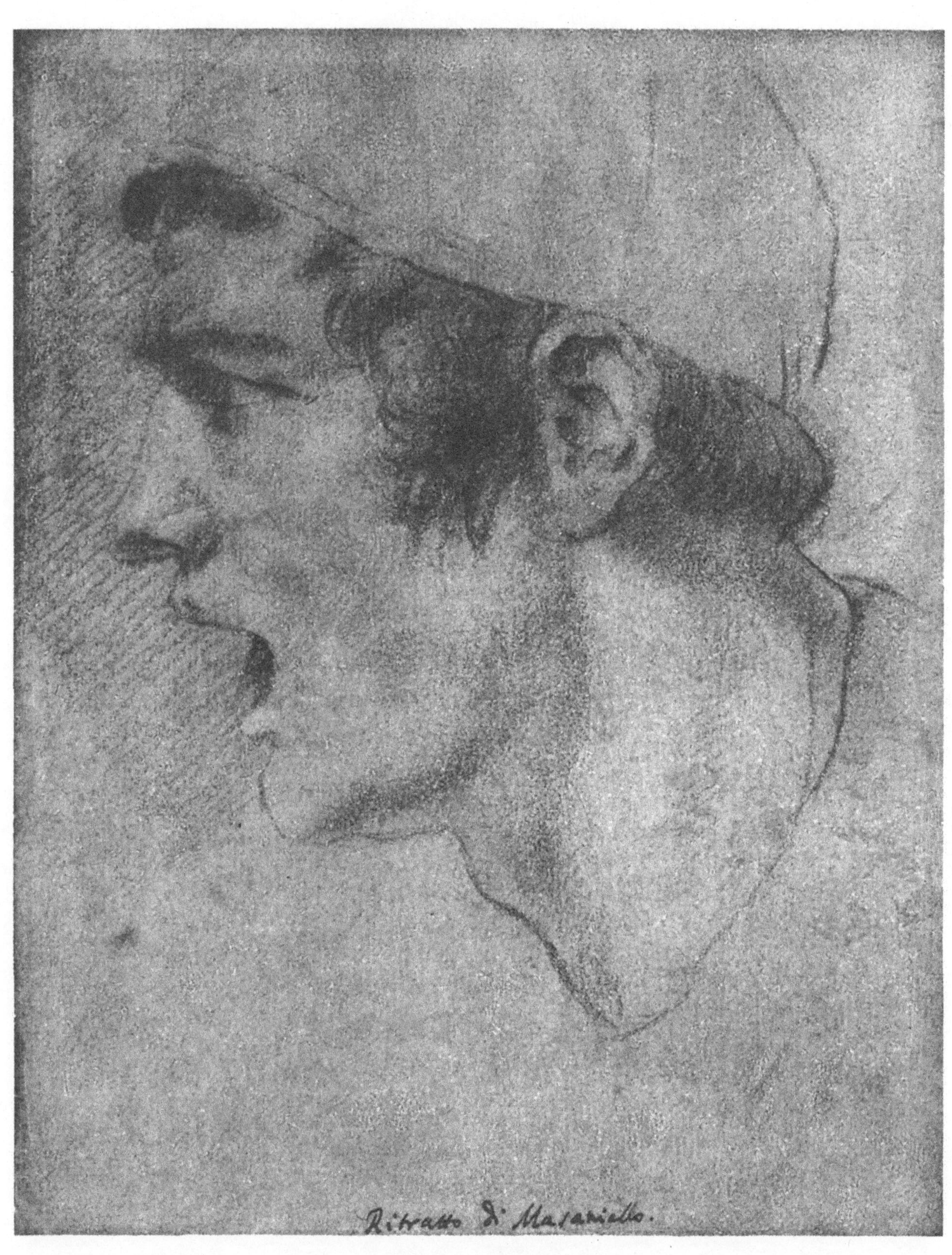

Aniello Falcone (1607–1656). Portrait of Masaniello (1620–1647).

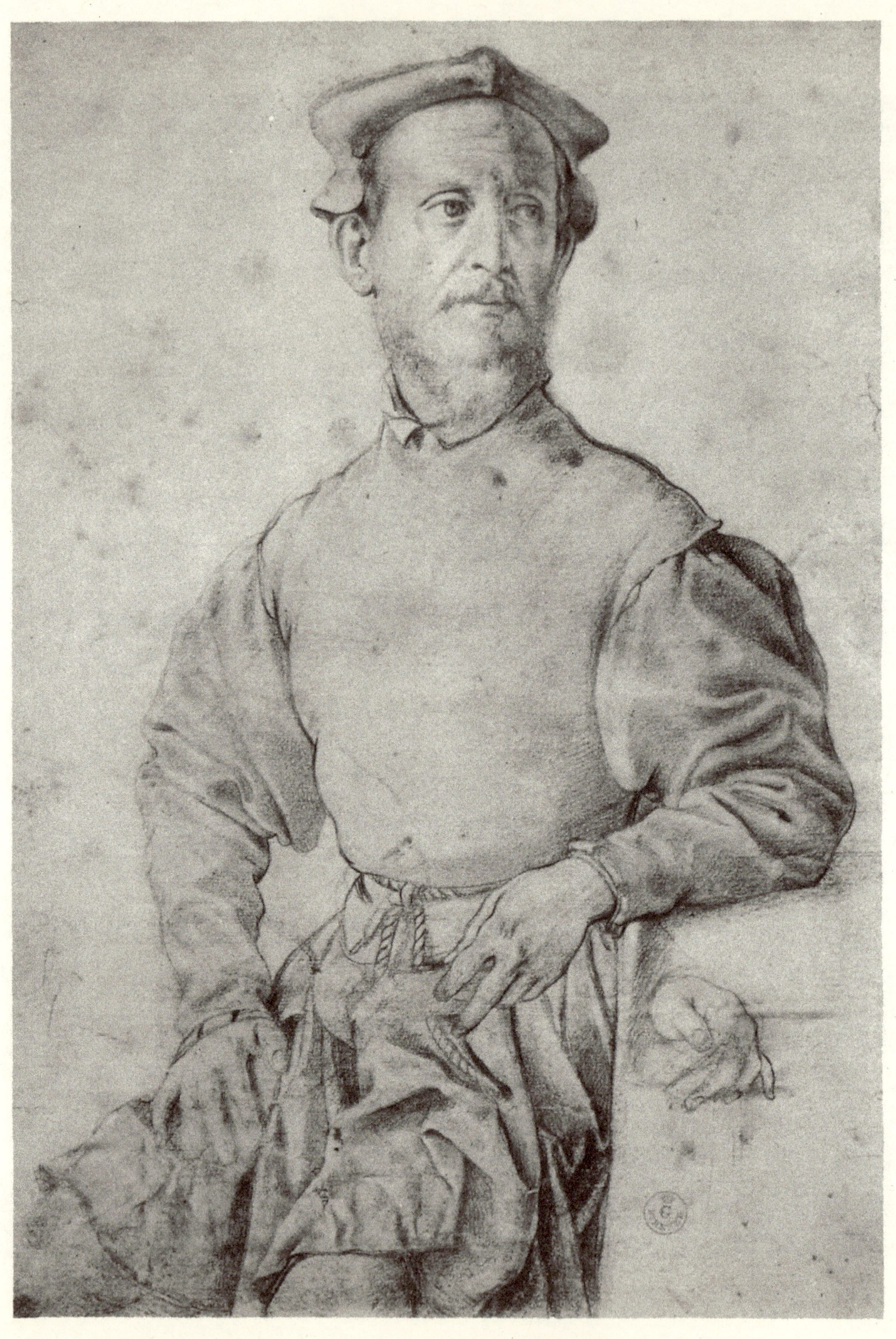

Pontormo (Jacopo Carrucci; 1494–1556/57). Mature man, seated. Black chalk. 387 × 256 mm.

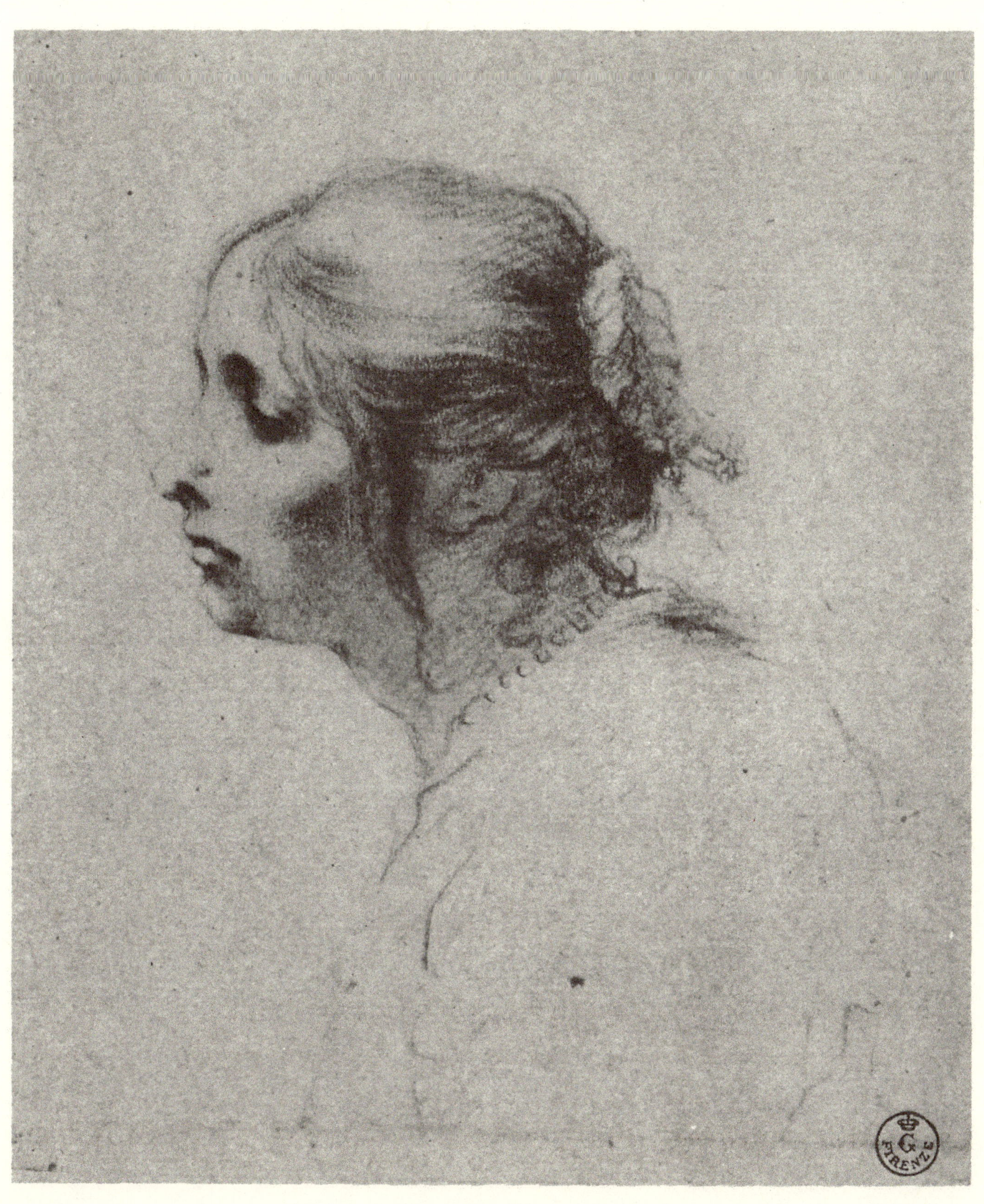

Francesco Furini (1604–1646). Head of a young woman. Red chalk. 225 × 200 mm.

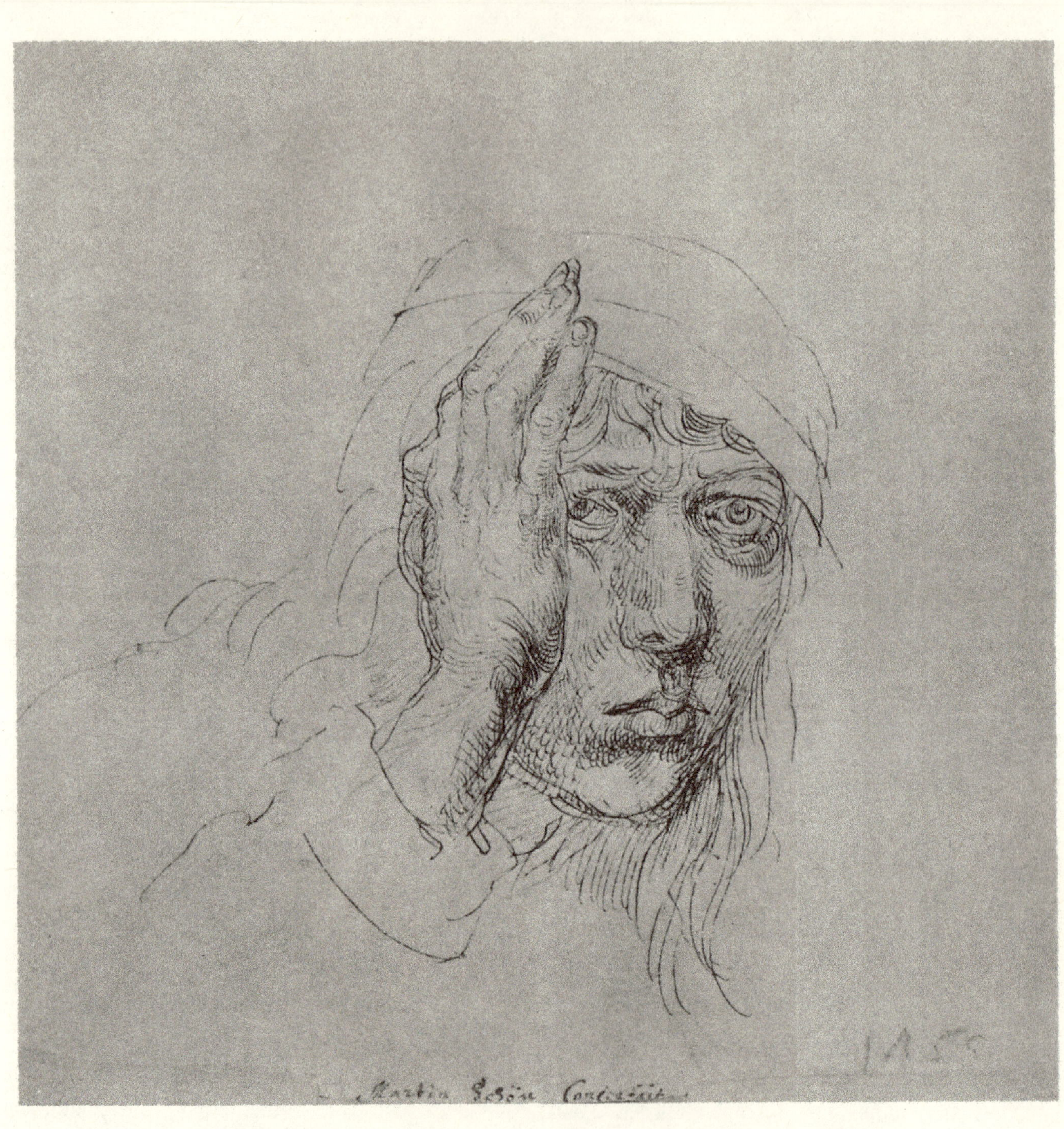

Albrecht Dürer (1471–1538). Self-portrait, ca. 1491. Pen and ink. 204 × 208 mm.

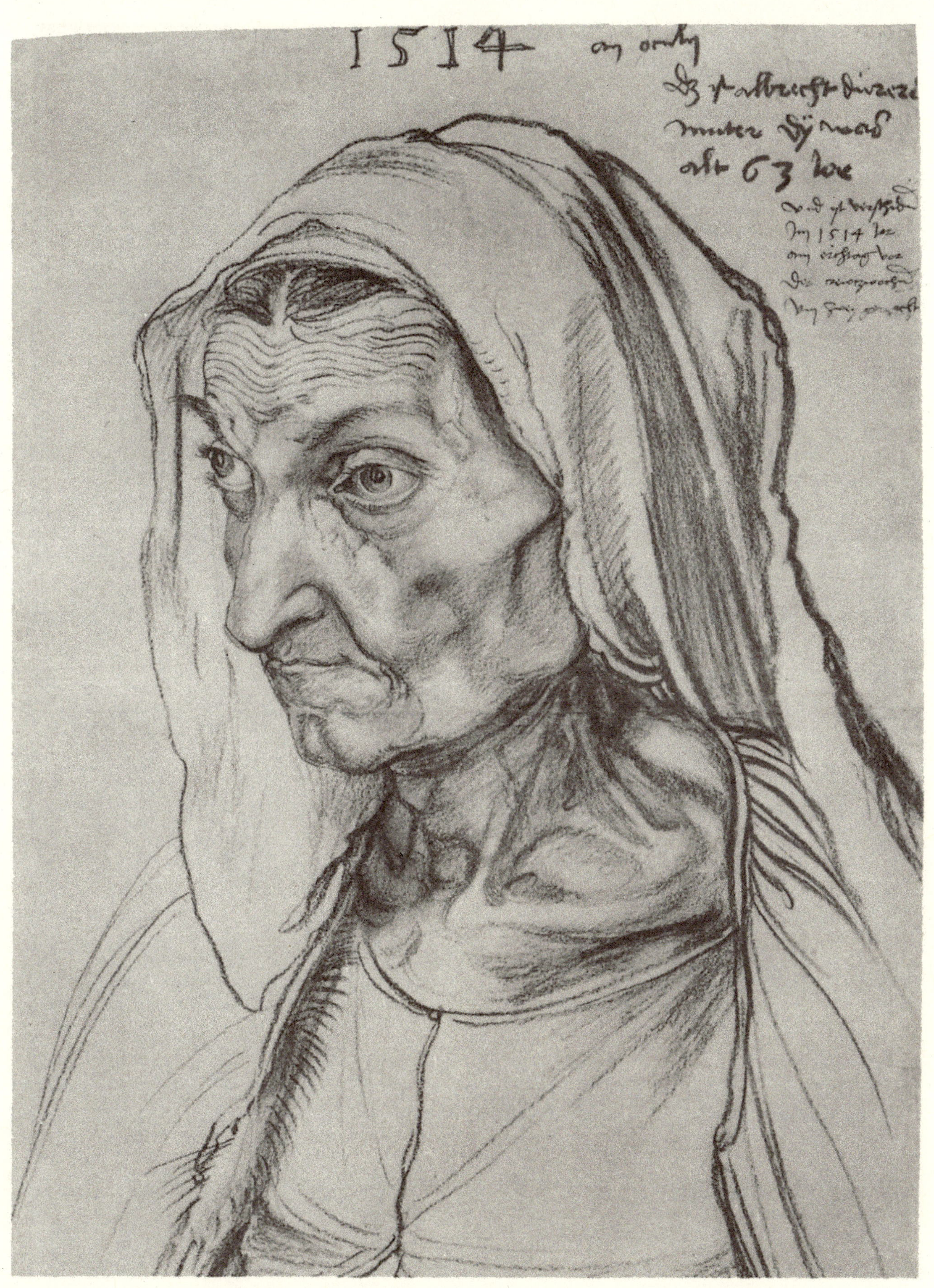

Albrecht Dürer (1471–1538). Portrait of the artist's mother, 1514. Charcoal. 421 × 303 mm.

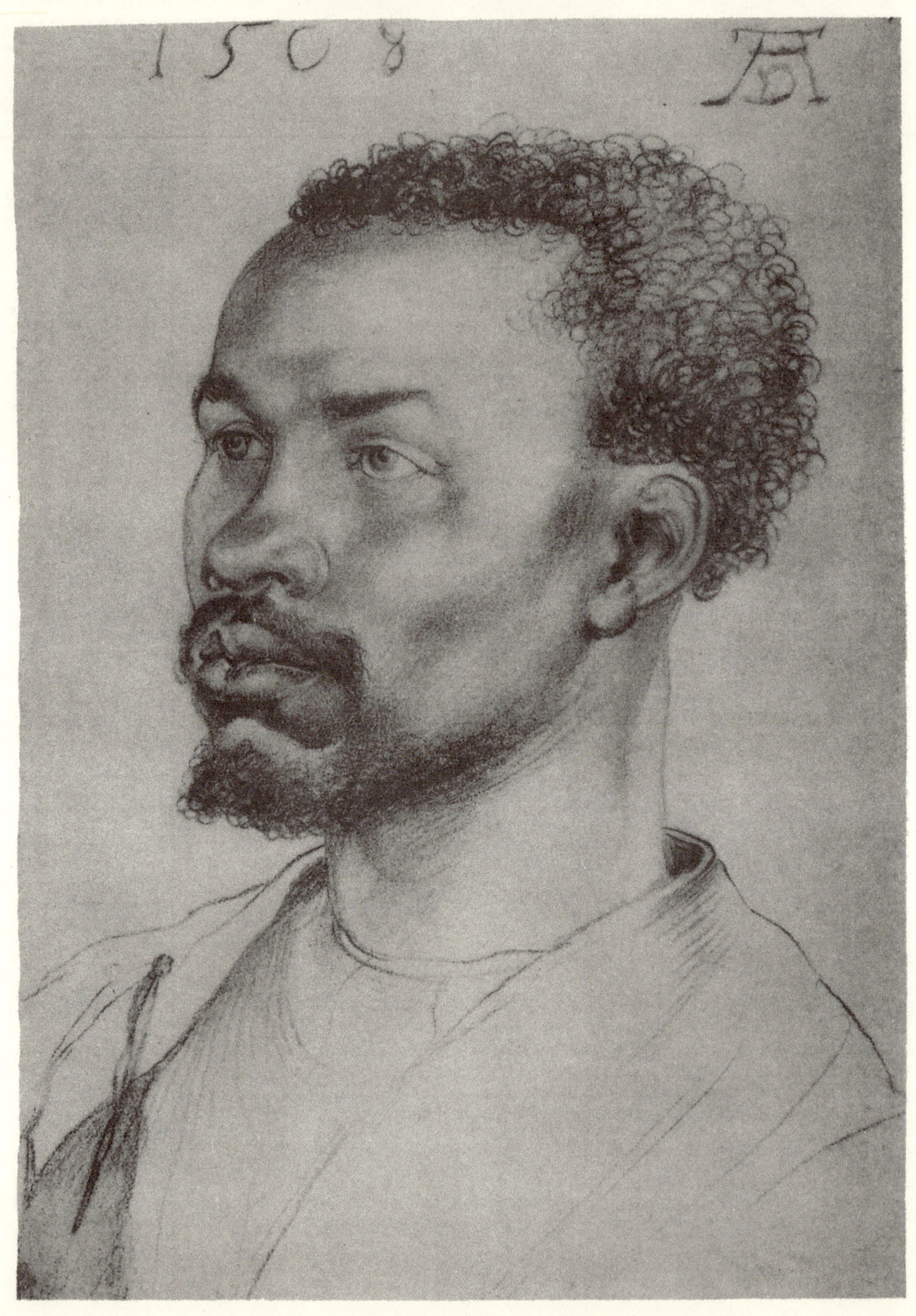

Albrecht Dürer (1471–1538). Head of a black, 1508. Charcoal. 320 × 218 mm.

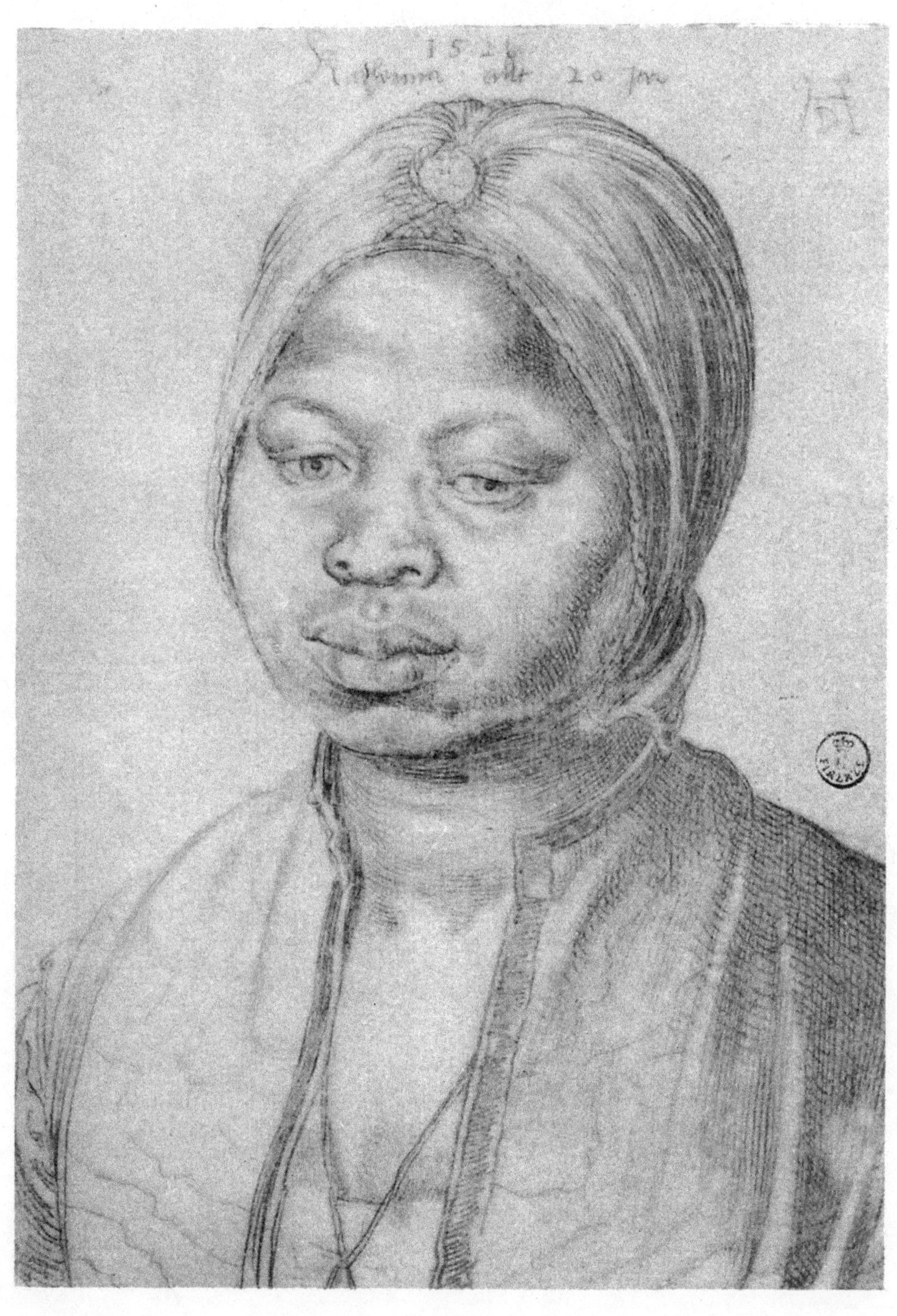

Albrecht Dürer (1471–1538). Portrait of a young Moor (Katherine, 20 years). Silverpoint. 200 × 140 mm.

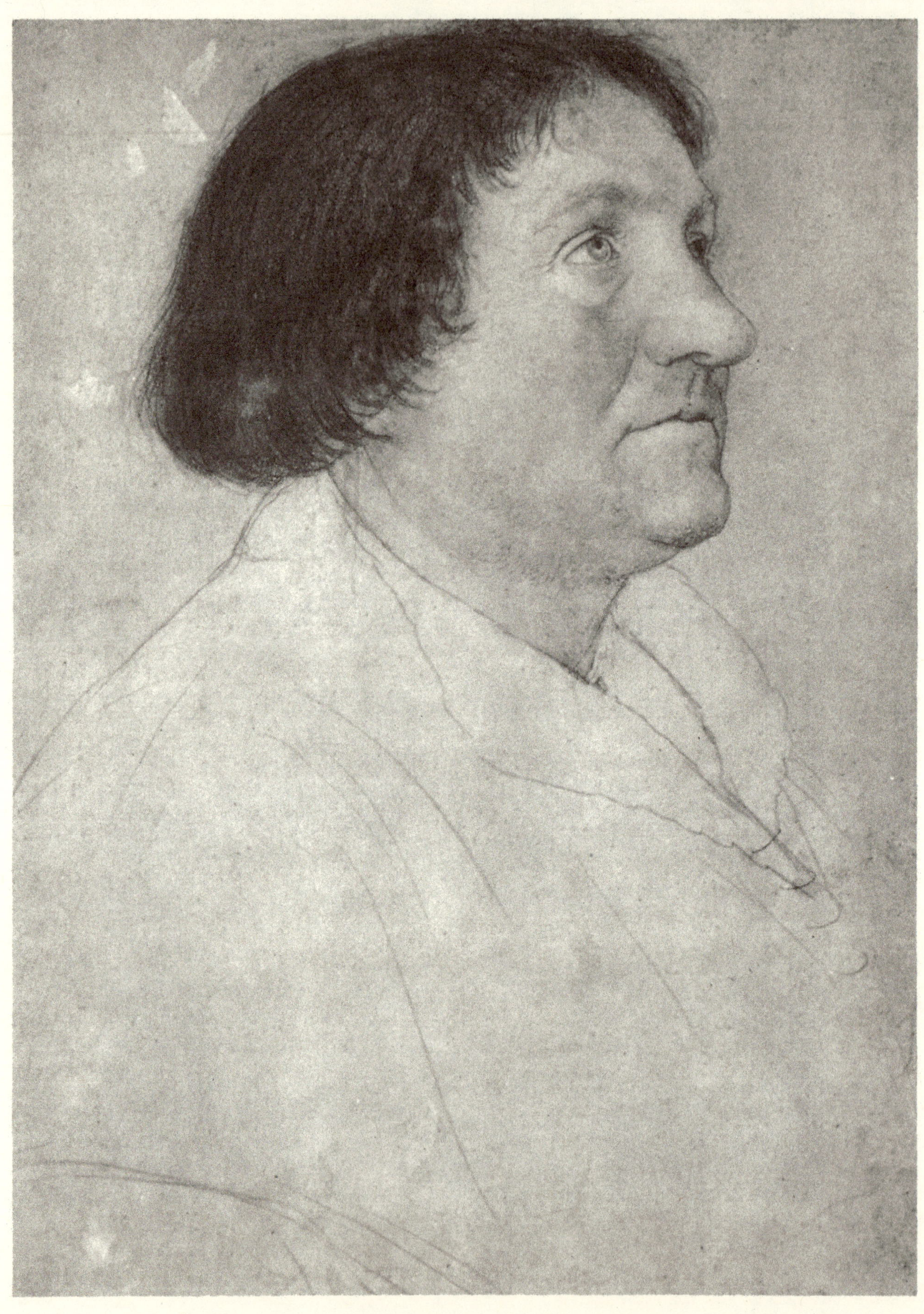

Hans Holbein the Younger (1497–1543). Portrait of the Mayor Jakob Meyer. Black and colored chalk. 383 × 275 mm.

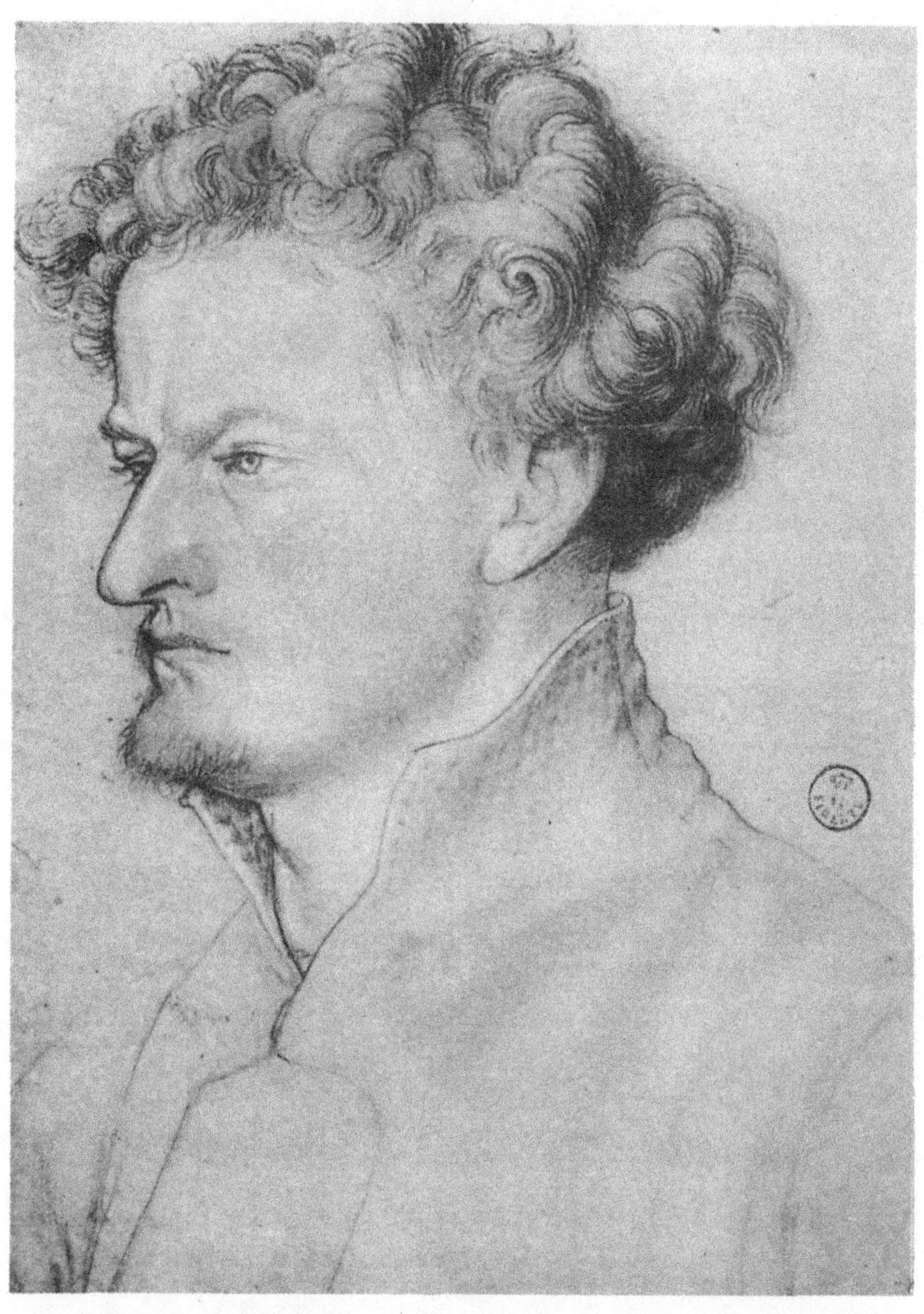

Hans Holbein the Younger (1497–1543). Portrait of a man. Silverpoint, red and white chalk on gray paper. 170 × 120 mm.

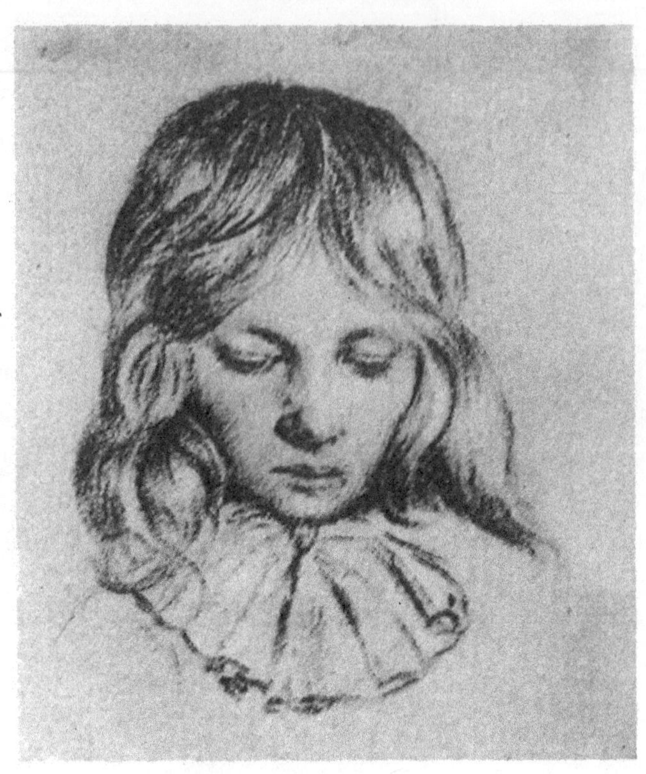

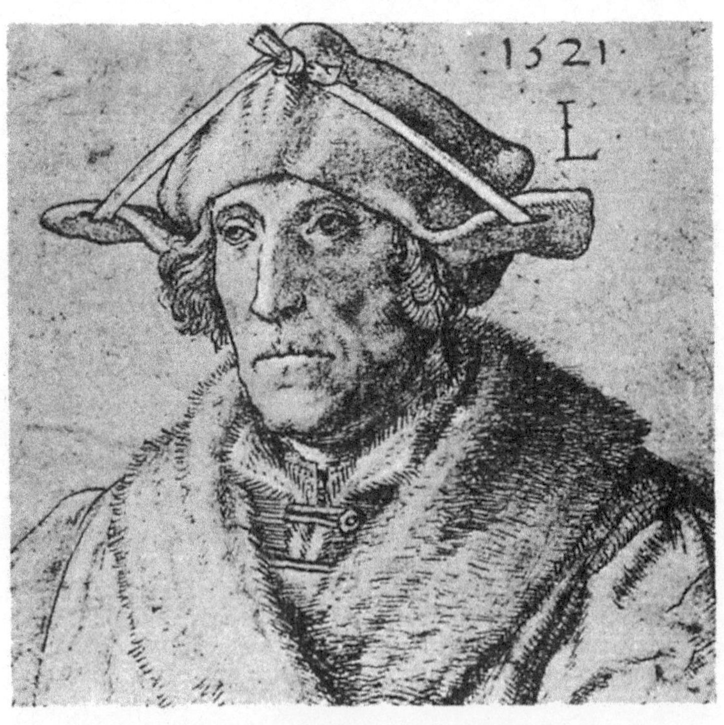

TOP: Gerhard Terborch (1617–1681). Portrait of a youth. Red chalk. BOTTOM: Lucas van Leyden (1489/94–1533). Portrait of Desiderius Erasmus (1466?–1536).

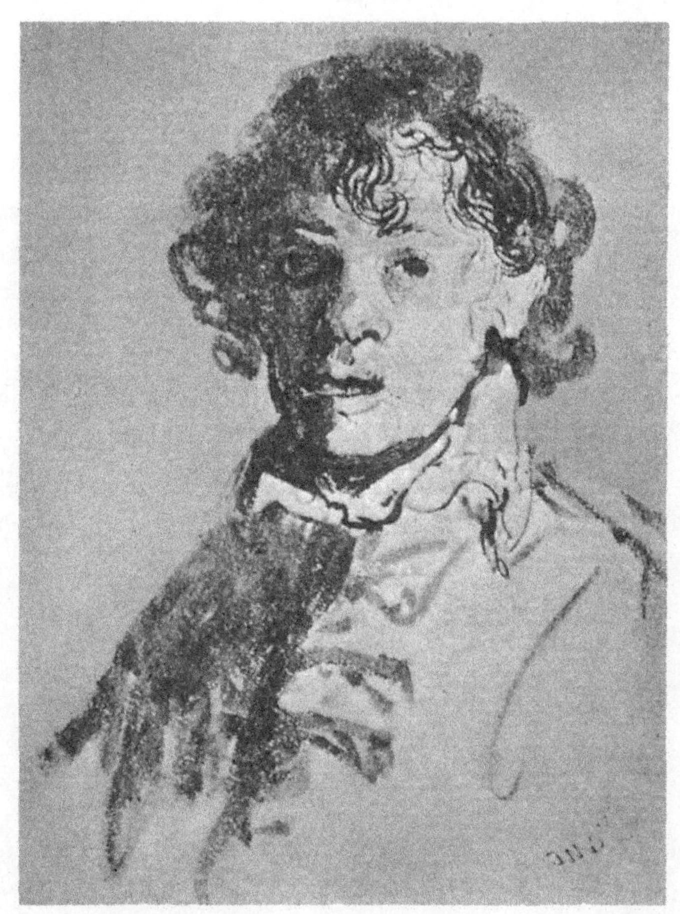

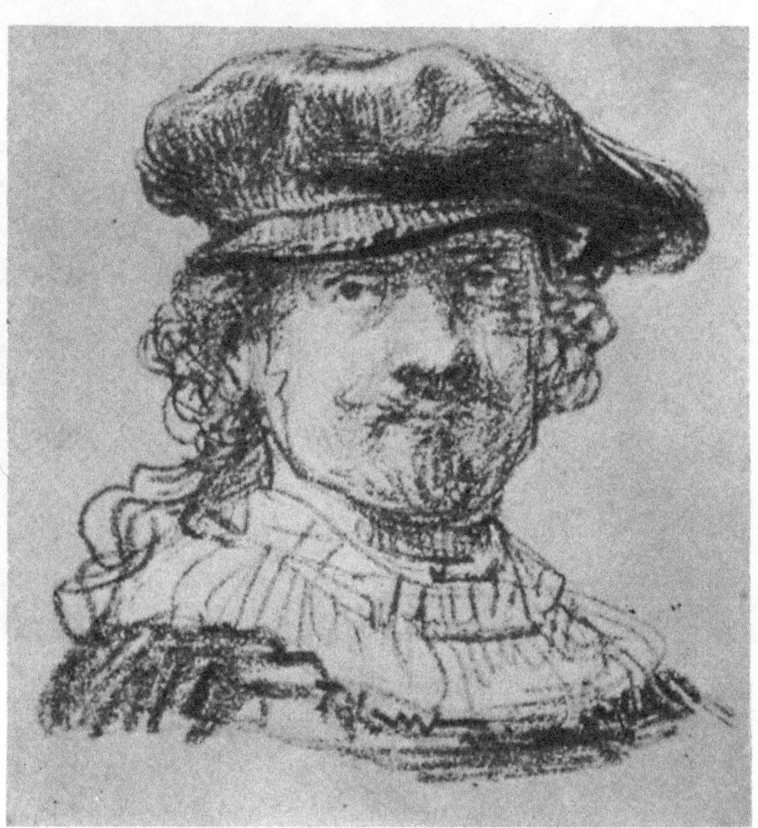

Rembrandt Harmenszoon van Rijn (1606–1669). TOP: Self-portrait. Pen and brown ink, brush and India ink. 127 × 95 mm. BOTTOM: Self-portrait. Red crayon. 129 × 119 mm.

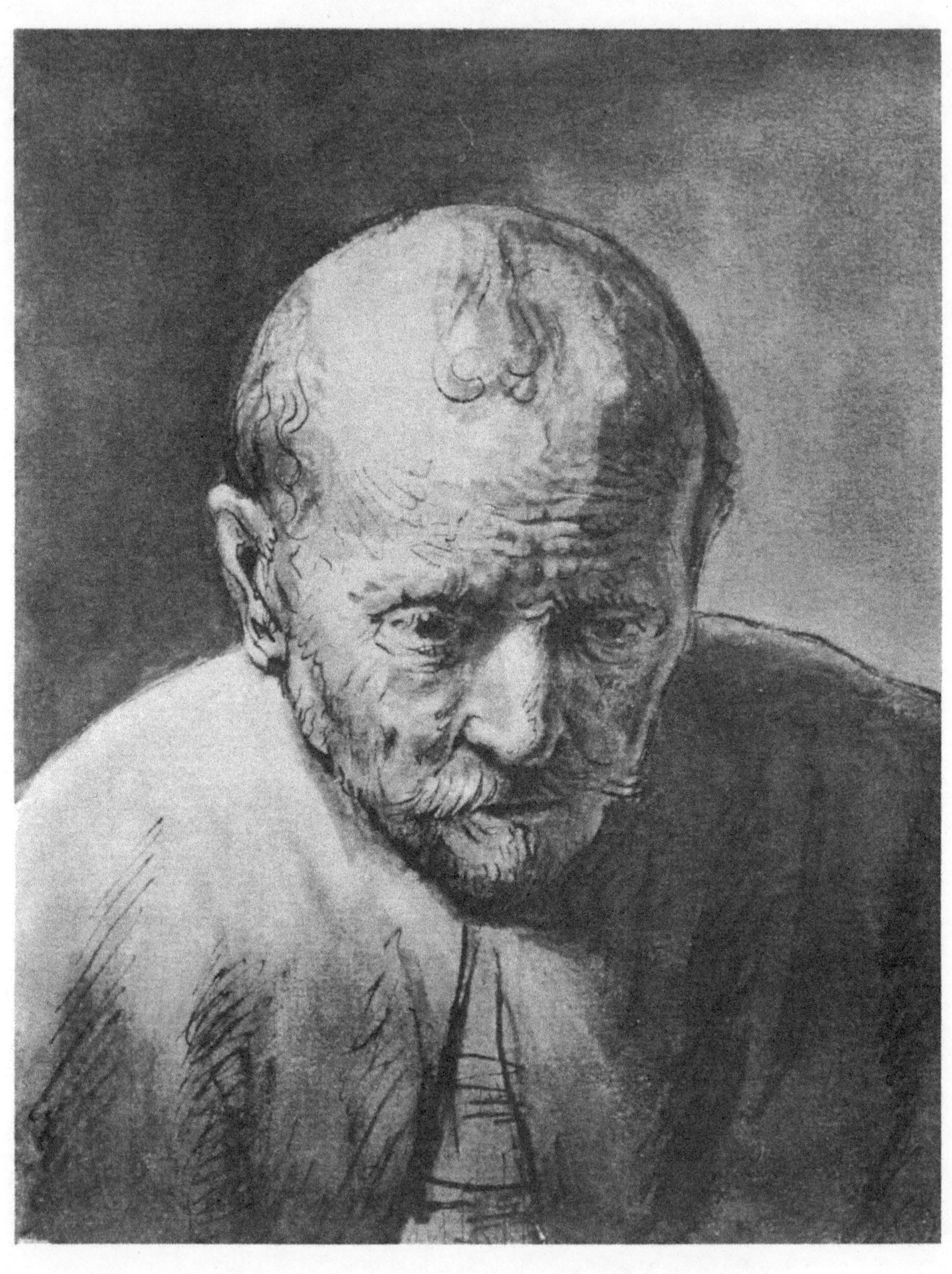

Rembrandt Harmenszoon van Rijn (1606–1669). Portrait of the artist's father. Pen and sepia, washed with India ink.

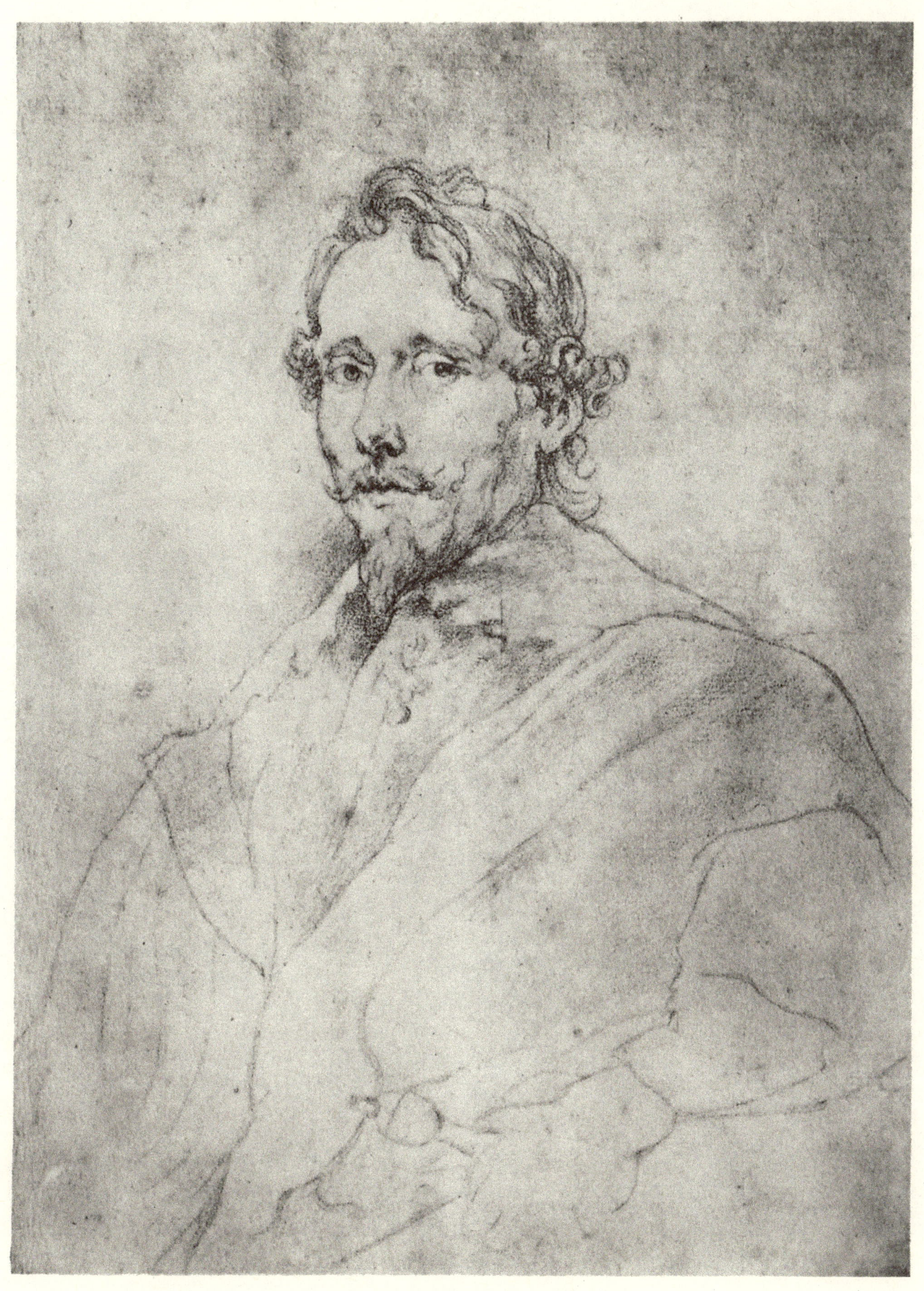

Anthony van Dyck (1599–1641). Philippe Le Roy, Lord of Ravels, state councillor to Philip IV of Spain. 260 × 190 mm.

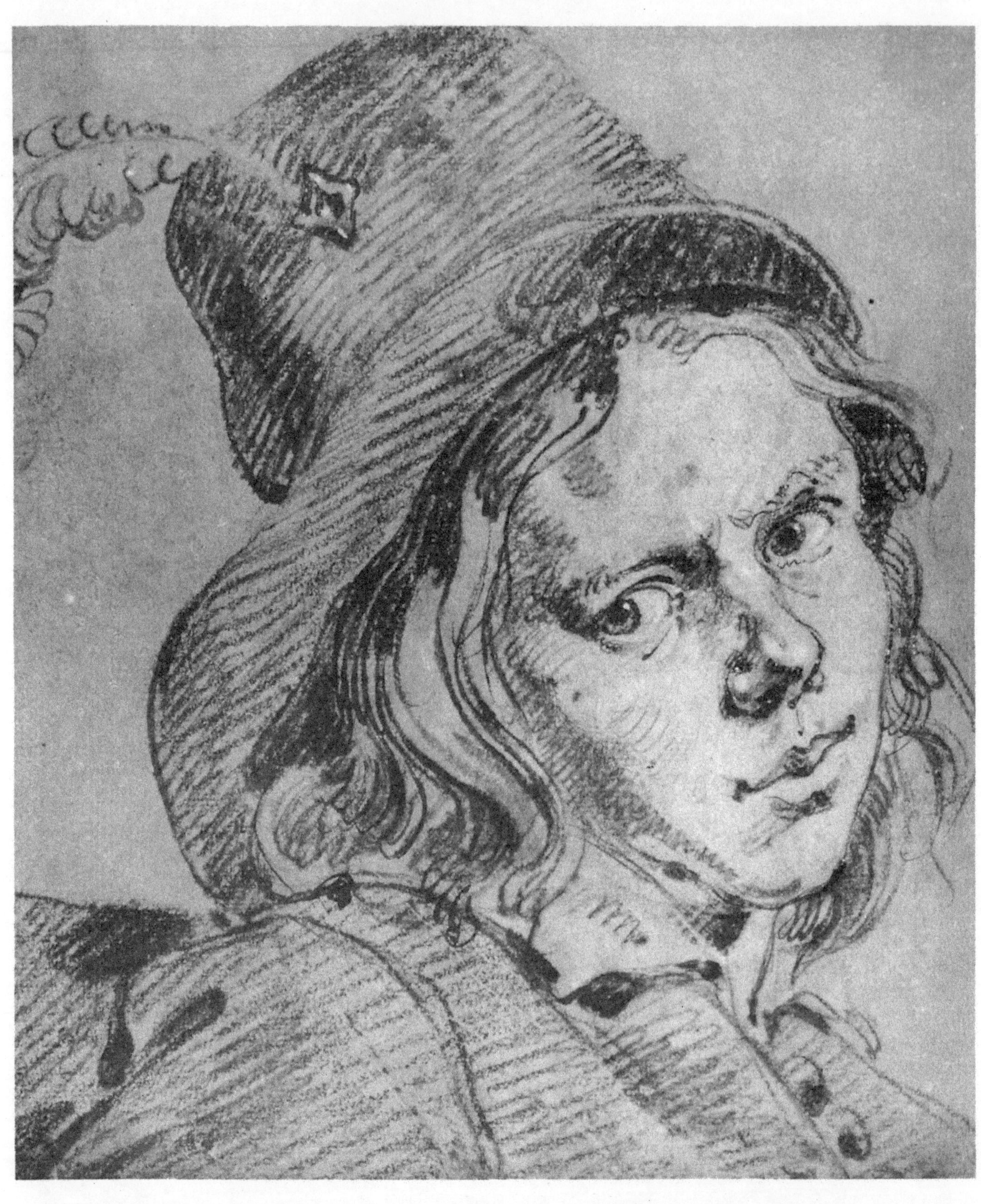

Frans Hals (ca. 1581–1666). Portrait of a youth.

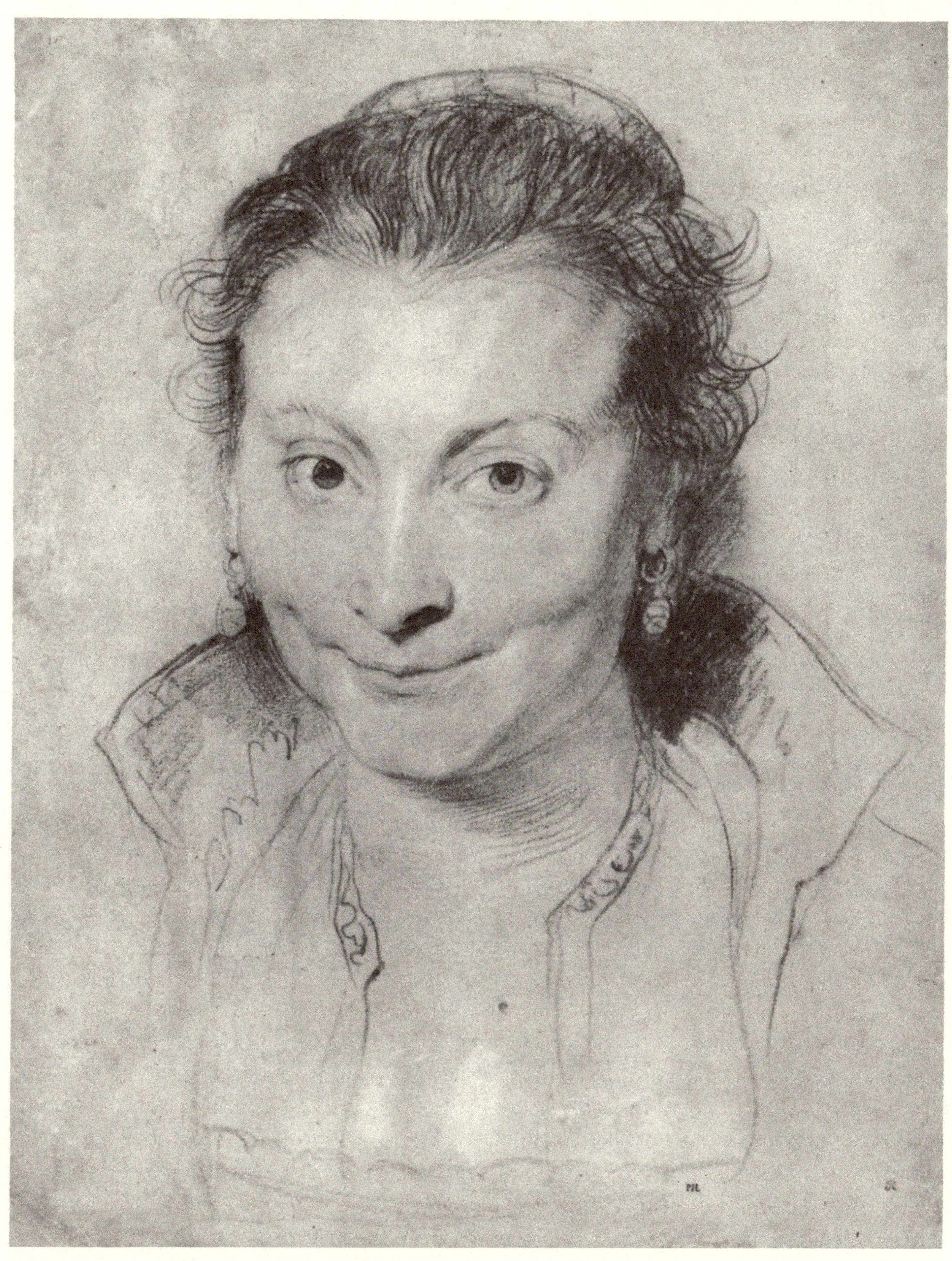

Peter Paul Rubens (1577–1640). Portrait of Isabella Brant, the artist's first wife (d. 1626). Black, red and white chalk. 381 × 292 mm.

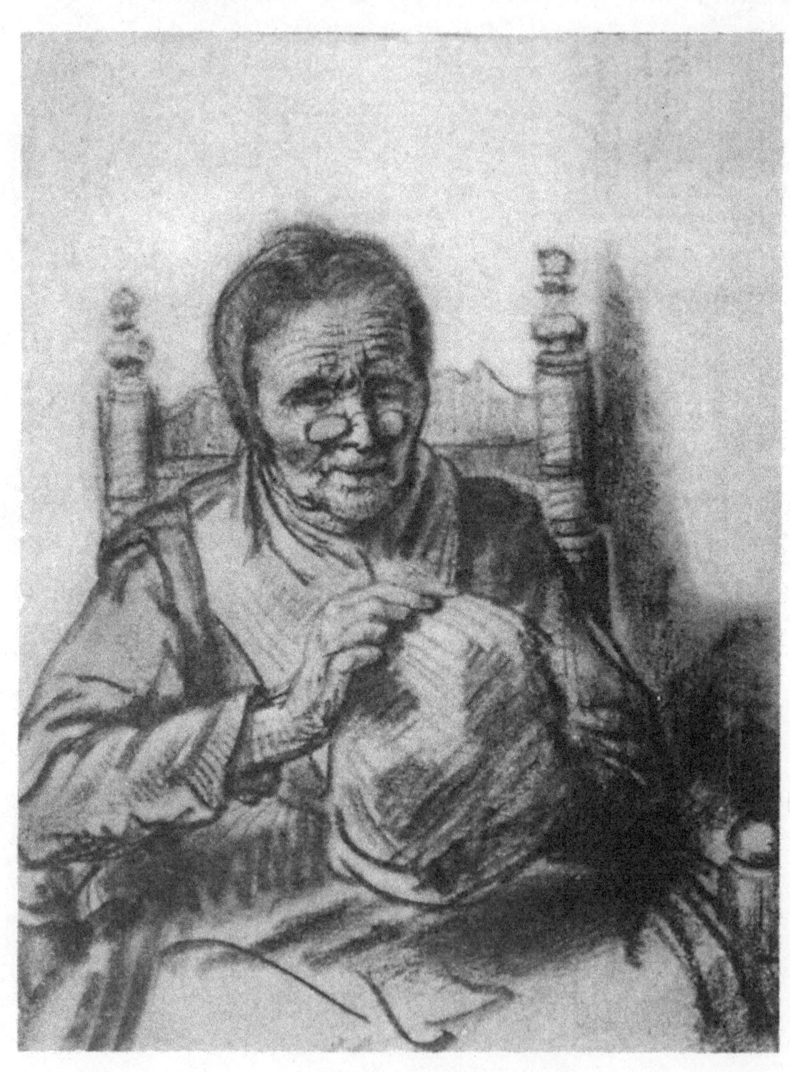

Nicolaes Maes (1634–1693). Portrait of an old woman.

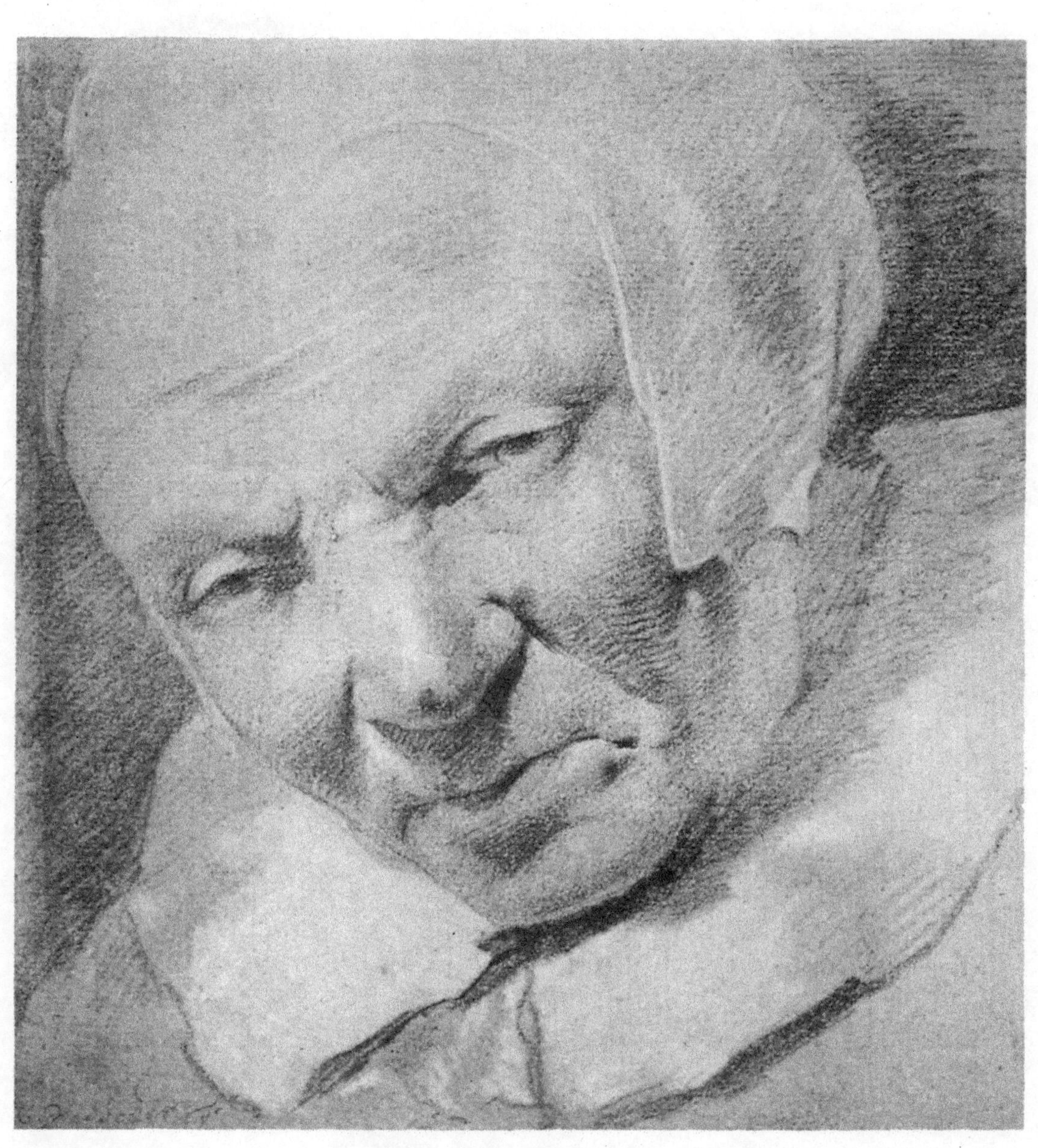

Cornelis Visscher (1619/29–1662). Portrait of an elderly woman.

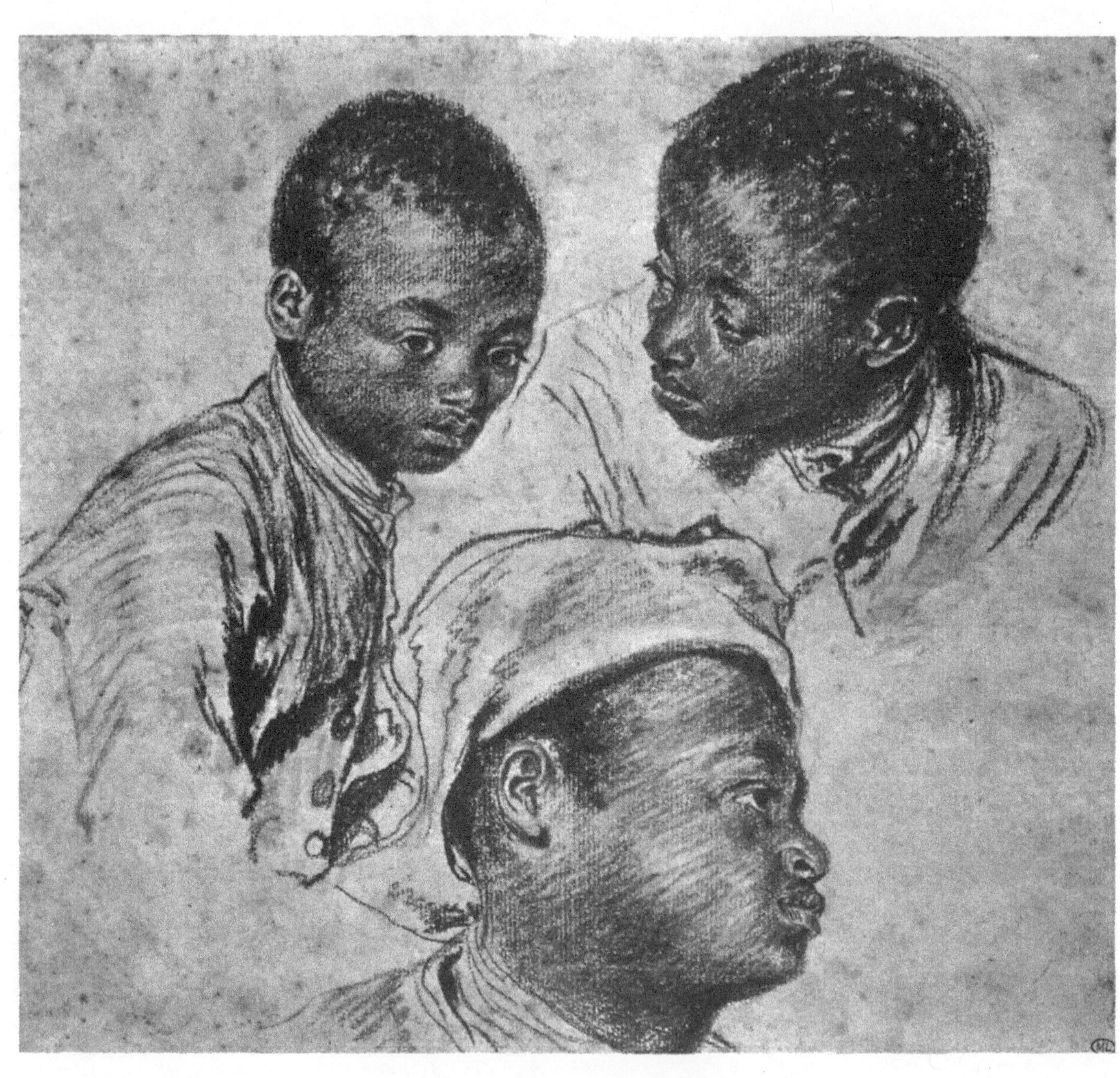

Antoine Watteau (1684–1721). Three studies of the head of a young black. Black and red chalk, white wash and watercolor. 243 × 271 mm.

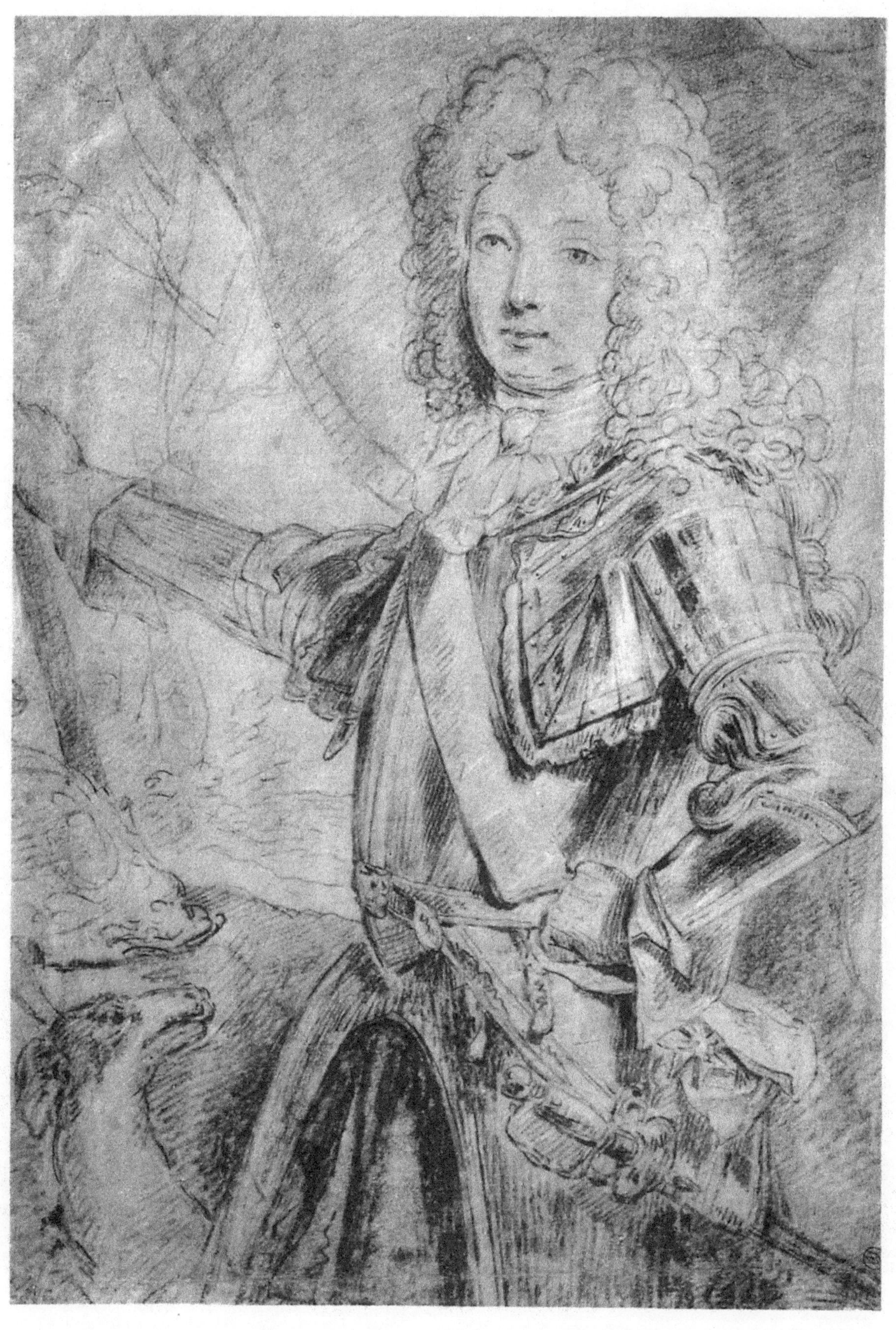

Hyacinthe Rigaud (1659–1743). The Duc de Noailles. Black chalk, heightened with white, on toned paper.

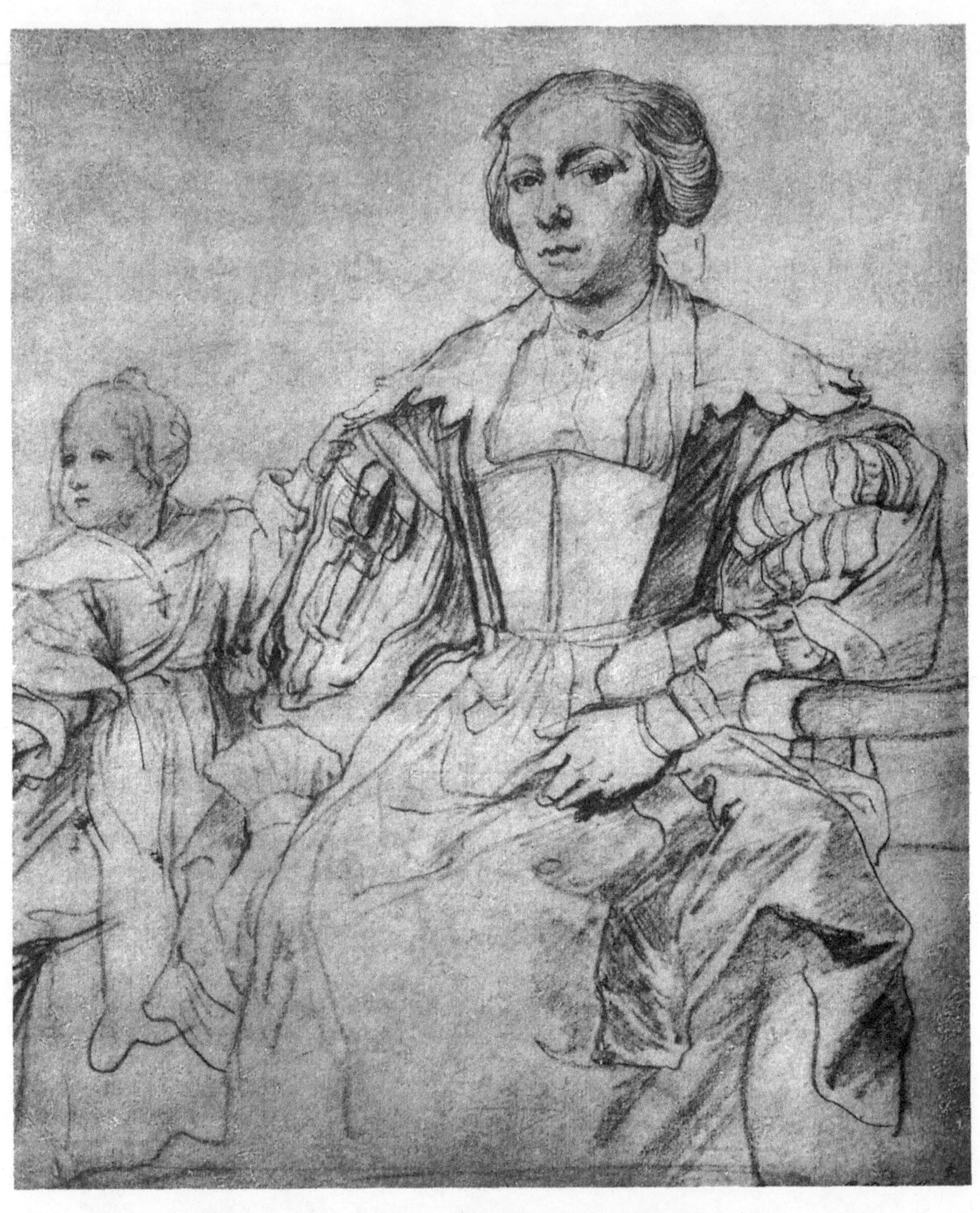

Anthony van Dyck (1599–1641). Portrait of a lady and a child. Black chalk.

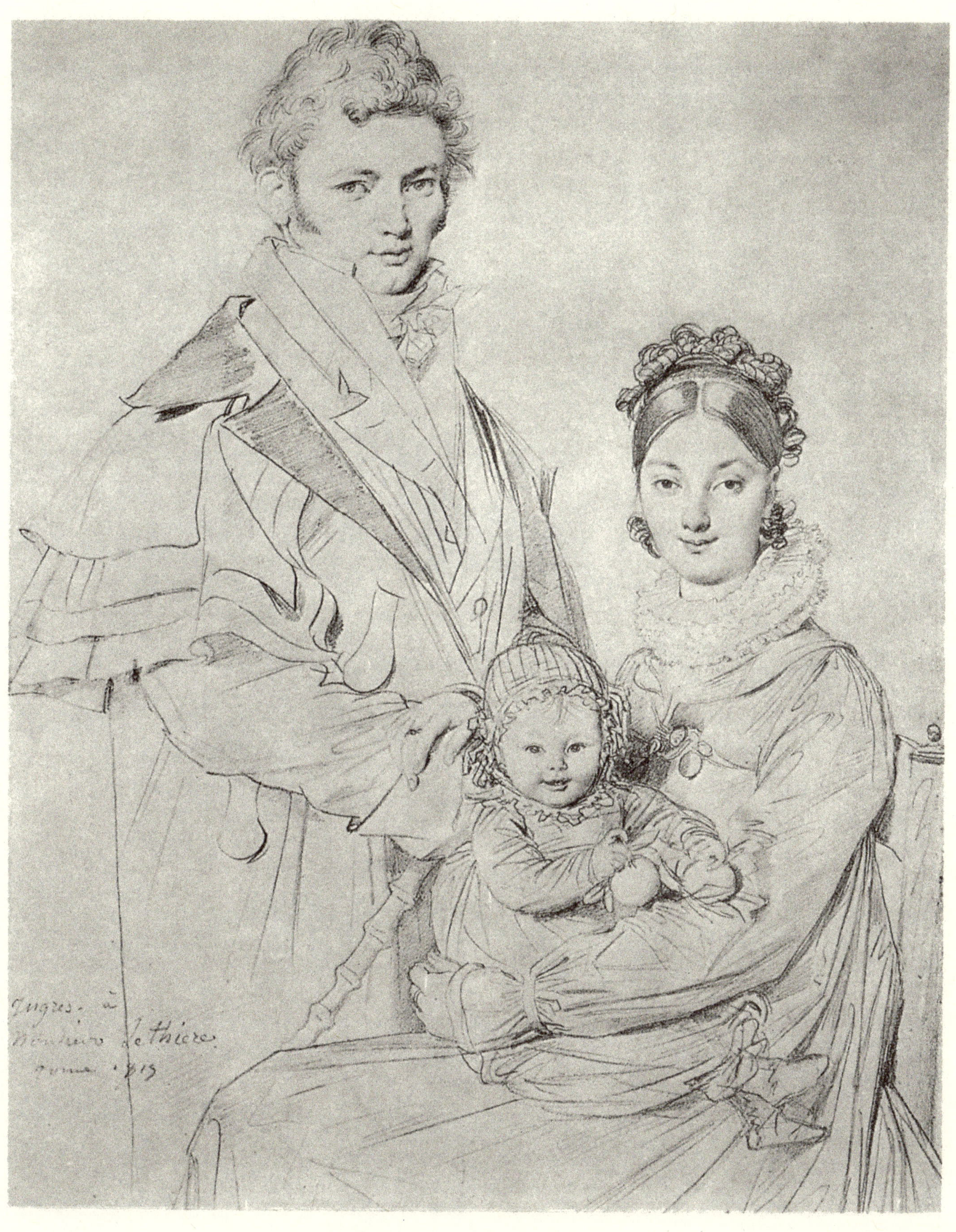

Jean-Auguste-Dominique Ingres (1780–1867). The Guillon-Lethière family, 1815. Pencil. 275 × 219 mm.

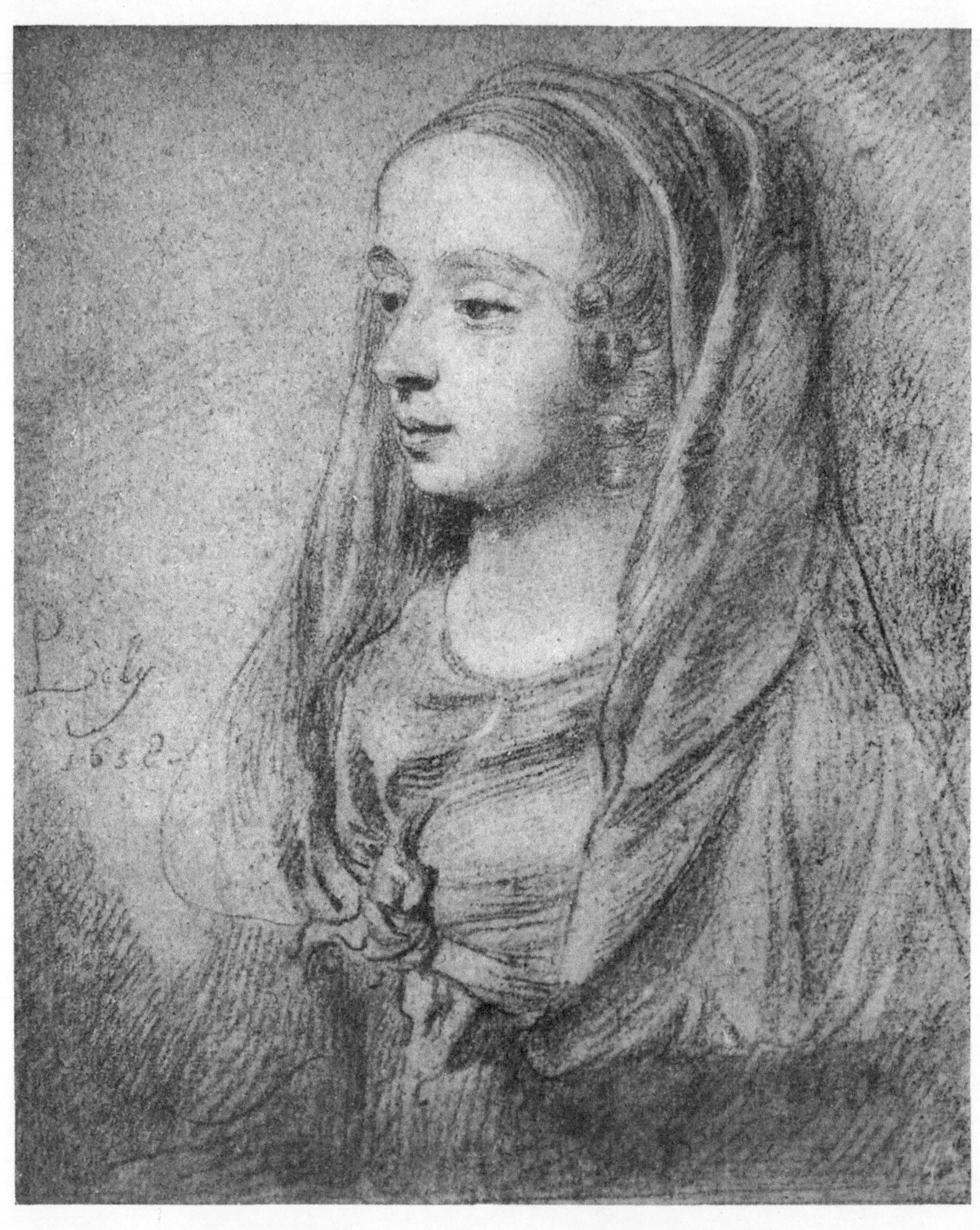

Peter Lely (1618–1680). Portrait of a lady. Black and white chalk on gray paper.